THE SUNDAY TIMES
Money Online

THE SUNDAY TIMES
Money Online

Matthew Wall

HarperCollins*Publishers*

Matthew Wall is a freelance journalist and TV research/producer best-known for his weekly *Web Wise* internet column in *The Sunday Times*. He also writes internet features for the paper's Culture section and has written several internet reports for business. He also advises companies on web design and strategy.

HarperCollins Publishers
77-85 Fulham Palace Road
Hammersmith
London W6 8JB

fireandwater.com
Visit the book lover's website

First published 2000

Reprint 10 9 8 7 6 5 4 3 2 1 0

© Times Newspapers Ltd 2000

ISBN   0 7230 1057 7

Designer: Sylvie Rabbe
Layout: Beatrice Waller
Editor: Charles Philips

Designed, edited and typeset by Book Creation Services Ltd.

Printed in Great Britain by Omnia Books Ltd, Glasgow G64

Contents

Chapter

Getting Started

Introduction

Welcome to *The Sunday Times Money Online* – the guide that helps you manage your money on the web and take control of your finances. In this guide we assume you're already pretty familiar with how the web works. If you're not, you should read *The Sunday Times Guide to the Internet* first to get yourself up to speed on the basics.

The financial services industry is developing so fast online that it is impossible to cover all the available money-related websites in this guide. New sites are being launched almost every day. And even the ones that are already up and running seem to be developing their services so fast that writing a guide is like trying to hit a moving target from an express train. So we've had to be selective, simply choosing the best. We've looked for quality and depth of information on offer, a high degree of transactional capability, plus a site design that is logical, attractive and easy to use.

Of course, you may not totally agree with our choices, or better sites may have been launched while the guide was being published, so we've made sure that you have plenty of pointers to other sources of information as well.

Why the rush online?

It seems that not a week goes by without some financial company announcing plans to move part or all of its business online, from banks to insurance companies, stockbrokers to mortgage providers. Some institutions are moving faster than others, but there is now a general recognition that this new medium is transforming the way we manage our finances. Product providers that don't go online risk being left behind completely.

Financial services are ideally suited to the web. After all, most financial products are actually just figures on a screen or page these days. With the rise of credit and debit cards and the ability to transfer money electronically, cash is playing a smaller and smaller part in our lives. And once financial products are reduced to a digital format they become far easier to distribute. Instead of sending cumbersome application forms and statements by post – a slow and inefficient process – product providers can send them across the internet in a few seconds.

The web has turned the world upside down. Before, financial companies had to spend millions of pounds sending out thousands of marketing leaflets and brochures. Now they can just tell potential customers their website address and people will come to them. You only need one brochure or application form on a website, yet it can be read by everyone. That's a big cost saving for a company and enables it to channel resources elsewhere – into customer service or lower borrowing rates and charges, for example. That's the beauty of the web.

The financial services industry is also moving online simply because that's the way more and more of us prefer to conduct our business. Companies are worried that if they don't offer their products this way, they'll lose out to competitors. And they're right. According to the latest research, around 15 million adults in the UK now regularly use the internet. Around 3.5 million of these are using the web to research and buy financial products.

So what's so great about the web?

There are many advantages to managing your money online. First and foremost, it saves time and hassle. If you're shopping around for a new mortgage, credit card, or personal loan you would normally have to spend hours on the phone or in the high street picking up leaflets in banks or building society branches. Then you would have the arduous task of trying to compare products, with all their confusing bells and whistles, looking for the best one.

The web gets rid of most of that legwork. Company websites are only a mouse click away. There's no standing in queues, no waiting for buses, no fears about vindictive traffic wardens. You do the research in the comfort of your own home at a time convenient to you.

And there are increasing numbers of websites that do most of the research for you, compiling databases of financial products and making it easy to compare them and sort them according to any number of criteria you choose. For example, when looking for a mortgage, some sites will let you specify whether you're after a fixed-rate or variable interest rate, how much you want to borrow and over what time, and whether you're happy to accept any compulsory insurances that come with it (*see* **Borrowing: Mortgages**, *page 95*). They will ignore all the mortgages that don't match your preferences, saving you time. This ability to sort and sift large volumes of data is something the web is extremely good at.

The web also helps you to keep bang up to date with your finances. In the bad old days, you might not have known that you were overdrawn until you received a letter or statement from your bank. By then you might have incurred interest penalties and even charges for the letter itself. With internet banking you can get an up-to-date balance whenever you like, and look through all your latest transactions. Most online banks will also allow you to transfer funds to other accounts electronically and pay bills online, too. You can even specify the date you want a bill to be paid – no more last-minute dashes to the bank or post office.

TIPS

With internet banking you can get an up-to-date balance whenever you like, and look through all your latest transactions.

This ability to keep up to date is a major advantage for investors. You can look up the very latest share prices and stock market news online, and keep pace in a fast-moving environment. You can get valuations of your portfolio whenever you want and buy and sell instantaneously at the click of a mouse.

Buying financial products online can also save you money. Many financial product providers find it cheaper to distribute their products online, direct to the customer. It cuts out the middleman – tied agents and independent financial advisers, for example – and they can pass on some of those savings to you. Online banks that have no branches to maintain can offer higher-than-average interest rates on savings, for example. Credit card providers can offer lower Annual Percentage Rates (APRs) for internet-only cards; insurance companies can offer discounts on policies bought over the web; and independent financial advisers can reimburse their usual commission on unit trust products because of the money they save by doing business online.

We're not at the stage yet where *everything* is cheaper online, so it still pays to try other channels, such as telephone brokers. But before too long the fruits of the web's efficiency will filter down to the customer for most product categories.

One indirect reason why the web helps save you money is that it leads to transparency in prices and conditions of financial services. If you're sitting in a branch or an office, a financial institution has you in its grasp. It's much easier to sell you its products because you're more likely to cave in and sign on the dotted line. For most of us, life's too short to be spending hours shopping around for the best product. It's enough that we actually got round to doing something in the first place.

But on the web, comparisons are so easy that the best product is much more obvious. And this means it's also much easier to spot uncompetitive companies selling overpriced products. They can no longer rely on the laziness of customers for their profits. This all leads to greater competition, and greater competition almost always means lower prices for customers. Isn't the web wonderful?

TIPS

Buying financial products online can save you money. Many financial product providers find it cheaper to distribute their products online direct to the customer – and they can pass on some of the savings to you.

Saving trees

Our economy is truly becoming digital, but we're not there yet. The need for written signatures is one of the main obstacles to achieving a totally paperless environment in financial services. Borrowing comes under the Consumer Credit Act, which was first passed in 1974 when the web was

5

just a twinkle in techies' eyes. The law stipulates that
loan agreements require a written signature. This means that
even cutting-edge websites have to revert to paper at some
point in the application process. These days you can get quite
far down the track – filling in a form and receiving an
agreement in principle online. But at some point you
usually have to sign something and post it off. This inevitably
slows things down.

But in 2000, the Government is introducing an Electronic
Commerce Bill which will give legal status to electronic or
digital signatures, doing away with the need for paper
altogether. These digital
signatures are not hand-
written signatures
transferred to a computer
screen like a logo. They are
clever bits of encryption
that can identify you and
your computer or mobile
device when you submit an
online application form.
They prove that the data sent across the web can only have
come from you and that no-one else has intercepted it or
meddled with it in transit. Digital signatures will make
researching, applying for and buying financial products a
seamlessly electronic process – saving time, effort and money.

But many people feel uneasy at the thought of a totally
paperless environment. Without some form of physical
evidence, they fear, proving ownership will be close to
impossible if there's a dispute or a company goes bust. This
is a legitimate concern, but there are fairly easy ways to deal
with the problem. For example, you can always print off
statements and completed application forms, and keep e-mail
correspondence as a record of your dealings with a product

TIPS

*Print off statements and completed
application forms, and keep e-mail
correspondence as a record of your
dealings with a product provider.
It is always useful to have a back-up
just in case.*

provider. It is always useful to have a back-up just in case. After all, the web isn't infallible and product providers also make mistakes from time to time.

Know your *info*mediaries from your *inter*mediaries

Before scouting round the web to find the best deal, it's important to know the different categories of service provider. It can be very confusing out there. You need to know whether you're being given advice, whether you're being shown all the products on the market and not just a selection, and whether the products on offer are unique to the web or available elsewhere.

Here's a quick run-through of the kind of services you'll come across and that we feature in this guide:

The company website
When companies first got wind of the web they would often just set up websites that were nothing more than online brochures, telling customers about their product ranges. Gradually they have begun to add more transactional features, such as the facility to apply online, and useful research features, such as calculators and general guides. Some companies have improved their online services to such an extent that you can go online and renew your car insurance, say, in a matter of minutes.

Where it gets confusing is that some companies have set up online-only ventures selling products that are different and often cheaper than those sold through branches or through sales forces and independent financial advisers. It's worth trying to find out what the situation is because you're not always guaranteed to get a product cheaper online. At least, not yet.

Of course, going to a company direct, whether online or via conventional channels, means that you only get to see its products, no-one else's. You don't know whether you're getting the best deal unless you compare its products with other companies. You can do this fairly easily by opening a new browser window and typing in a rival company's web address so that you can look at the product particulars side by side, but this is still a fairly time-consuming and cumbersome process. It is far quicker to go to an independent site that surveys the whole market, or at least a good proportion of it.

Infomediary

This is the simplest but often the most useful kind of website. It provides information to consumers to help them make decisions about their finances. Some specialize, concentrating on mortgages or investments, for example, others cover personal finance in general – everything from personal loans to tax-planning. You'll normally be able to compare and contrast financial products and services, receive news and read up about specific subject areas. Some just provide relevant news and research resources.

Such sites normally make their money through advertising, but they can also earn commission from financial companies if a customer clicks on a link, goes through to that company and takes out a product with them. Sometimes they also charge for a certain level of service, such as live share prices or stock market news, but most of the information is free.

Infomediaries don't provide individual advice and for this reason they don't usually make specific product recommendations. But they can provide general advice through online subject guides, in much the same way that newspapers do.

The trend is for infomediaries to increase the links with companies mentioned on their websites. For example, if you're looking for a credit card you might go to a general personal finance infomediary website and look up the lowest APR rates. If you like what you see and you want to apply, you would normally have to leave the infomediary website and either ring up the card provider or go to its website to apply online, if it offers that facility.

But increasingly infomediaries are including links to product providers on their websites. This makes it easier for customers to select a product and then click straight through to the provider. If the provider is really clued up, the customer will be able to apply online there and then, making it possible to research and buy a product in a matter of minutes.

> **WARNING**
>
> *Infomediaries may not cover the whole market for a particular product. Don't assume that the 'best buy' table is the last word.*

Due to the general nature of these sites, they do presuppose a level of knowledge on the part of the user. For example, you might be able to compare and contrast all the available fixed-rate mortgages on an infomediary site, but it might not be very good at telling you whether this kind of mortgage is right for you in the first place.

Another point to be aware of is that infomediaries may not cover the whole market for a particular product. Some product providers don't allow their product details to be included on some sites. So you shouldn't assume that the 'best buy' table, showing all the lowest rates, whether for personal loans or credit cards, is the last word. It pays to check a few other sites as well, including the providers own.

Infomediaries can save you time shopping around but it is still too early to say whether you'll always get the best deal via these sites.

Intermediary offering individual advice

The most common type of intermediary is the independent financial adviser (IFA), who will look at your individual financial circumstances in their entirety and recommend specific products to suit you. Independent financial advisers are duty bound to survey the entire market. Some have set up websites purely as a marketing tool. After all, the web is a great way for a local adviser to advertise to a national audience. Others have gone further and offer discounts if customers transact with them via the web. They feel they can pass on some of the cost savings achieved from marketing themselves more efficiently in this way.

As we went to print, there was only one IFA that offered individual financial advice online. Customers fill in and submit a detailed 'fact find' questionnaire, and the IFA then makes recommendations via e-mail. This kind of service is likely to become more common, with the IFAs carrying out the application process online via their own links to providers, or leaving it up to the customers to do it. And before too long, when high-speed internet access becomes widespread, there's no reason why we won't be able to have one-to-one video consultations with IFAs using web cameras (webcams) sitting on top of our computers.

One thing is for sure: the web, with its wealth of free, detailed financial information, is forcing IFAs to buck up their ideas and work harder to justify their commissions and fees. The web has made it much easier for ordinary people to educate themselves about available products and make more informed decisions. Although there is still a need for independent financial advice in a number of areas, the ability of the customers to do their own research has raised serious questions about the extent of IFAs' future role.

It becomes more confusing when a large IFA uses its influence to repackage providers' products for its own customers. In this case you're being offered products that you can't get from the providers directly. But it is then difficult to know whether you're dealing with a truly independent adviser or just another product provider. The provision of mortgages is one area in which this is happening more often, since mortgage advice isn't so heavily regulated as other areas of personal finance.

Intermediary without advice

This hybrid category of website usually offers products that are its own versions of providers' products tailored for an internet audience. The site doesn't profess to offer any independent advice, but it does sell products or services, unlike most infomediaries. If you buy a product via this kind of intermediary you become its customer, rather than a customer of the underlying product provider – if there is one.

Most online stockbrokers would fit into this category, given that they carry out share trades on your behalf on an 'execution-only' basis – that is, without advice. Yet you pay the broker for the service and it normally holds your shares for you in a nominee account; *see* **Investing**, *page 47* for more on this.

To sum up . . .

If you're confused by all these categories, I don't blame you. It doesn't help that the distinctions between them are becoming more blurred by the day. But it is important to know what kind of site you're dealing with. Here's a checklist of questions to ask yourself when you're perusing a financial website:

- Is it simply an information provider or is it trying to sell me products?

- If it's just an information provider, how much of the market does it really cover?

- Is it a single company offering only its own products, or an intermediary (broker) offering a range of products?

- Are the products offered by an intermediary unique to it or could you get the same direct from a product provider?

- Are you getting general advice or individual advice based on a detailed understanding of your particular financial circumstances?

See **Protection**, *page 129* for more information on how you can check that websites are qualified by the financial regulators to offer the kind of services they do.

Chapter 2

Banking

Introduction

Online banking has really taken off over the past couple of years. We've seen big 'bricks-and-mortar' banks move online in droves, some even launching internet-only offshoots, usually with silly names. We've also witnessed the arrival of Europe's first full internet-only bank, and the hype surrounding web-enabled mobile phones.

Banks have taken a relatively long time embracing the internet, largely because they've only recently invested millions in developing call centres in response to the telephone banking revolution. At last they seem to have realized that the net is here to stay and that if they don't get a move on customers may well migrate to rival banks that do offer internet banking.

And the threat doesn't just come from other UK banks. Supermarkets, insurance companies, stockbrokers – virtually anyone – can open an internet bank, not to mention European and American banks looking to expand into new markets. The internet's global reach and increased regulatory integration – especially in Europe – will make international banking easier. If you've got a well-known brand, there's no reason why you can't sell financial products on the web – just look at Virgin. The whole shape of the financial services industry, for so long set in its ways, is being transformed by the internet, and the public likes it.

The number of European internet banking sites had reached more than 1,200 by the end of 1999, reflecting the demand for such services. UK researcher Datamonitor predicts that there will be around 2 million UK internet banking customers by the end of 2000, rising to nearly 5.5 million by 2004, the largest single-country proportion of Europe's predicted total of 21 million internet banking customers. Fletcher Research, another UK research company, thinks that more than 9 million users will be banking online by 2004.

The rise of internet-enabled mobile phones – called Wireless Application Protocol or WAP phones – will help boost the numbers of people banking online. We'll be able to see mini-statements on our phone handsets or on the larger screens of our hand-held organizers. Voice-recognition software will enable us to speak commands into our phones rather than having to type them in on the fiddly numeric keypad. Interactive digital television beaming directly into the nation's living rooms will also extend electronic banking to the mass market.

FUTURE TRENDS

The rise of internet-enabled mobile phones – called Wireless Application Protocol or WAP phones – will help boost the numbers of people banking online. We'll be able to see mini-statements on our phone handsets or on the larger screens of our hand-held organizers.

We are also likely to see the extension of internet access into bank branches, so that you'll be able to pop in and look up your latest statement, set up some bill payments and maybe transfer some money between accounts, without having to queue to see the cashier.

Security fears that have prevented many people from transacting over the net will largely disappear. Financial services companies tend to be quite advanced in this area anyway, and they generally use 128-bit encryption, which is a very secure way of scrambling data before it crosses the network. You can be almost certain that no-one can intercept your bank details while they're in transit. As long as you are careful about protecting your user name and password, security shouldn't be an issue any more.

'Direct-dial' banking versus internet banking

When banking via PCs first started out it involved the bank providing you with software that you had to load on to your home computer. Your modem would than dial up the bank direct and your PC would communicate with the bank's computers. In other words, you didn't have full internet access. To go on to the internet you had to disconnect from the bank and redial via your internet service provider. There were, and still are, some advantages to this – the main one being that you're not prey to the internet's traffic jams at busy times of the day.

But the main drawback of direct-dial banking was that it was not flexible enough to cope with customers online financial needs. For example, supposing you had an online sharedealing account and you wanted to top it up with funds from your bank account. You could go online, click through to your stockbroker and investigate your account to see how much cash you had to spare for further investment. While still online, you could then open a new window in your web browser and click through to your internet bank, check your balance and decide how much you could afford to transfer. You could carry out the instruction there and then if you wanted. With direct-dial banking you would have to have logged on, then off, then on and off again.

Another disadvantage of direct-dial banking was that banks would have to send all their customers new software if they wanted to upgrade the service. People would inevitably have problems loading it and ring up for help. The whole business was proving too costly and cumbersome. With internet banking, the bank can update its website whenever it likes and automatically load the latest versions of any necessary software onto customers' PCs while they're online. It's just more efficient.

Internet banking also means you can access your account from any wired-up computer in the world. It gives you mobility and control. With direct-dial banking you're tied to the computer on which you've loaded the software. At the time of writing there were just a few banks continuing to offer direct-dial banking, with the majority offering full internet banking. For the purposes of this guide, we've concentrated on those that offer internet banking. It's the future.

Of course, greater flexibility for customers is a double-edged sword. The internet gives consumers the chance to compare rival products and services much more easily. For once, it's the customer that's in control of the banking relationship, not the bank manager. An uncompetitive service is more obvious on the net because comparisons are much easier to make.

So what's so great about banking on the internet?

First of all it's important to point out that there are different types of internet banks offering different levels of service. Some specialize in savings accounts, mortgages and credit cards, others provide the full suite of banking services, including cheque book and cash card. Some are backed by big parent companies, others are stand-alone start-ups. Below we give a sketch of the range of services on offer, but not all of the banks offer the whole lot.

The main advantage of banking online is that you get access to your account information whenever you want. You're no longer restricted to bank opening hours. You can get an up-to-date account balance and review all your most recent transactions – up to six months' worth in some cases. And the visual format is much more helpful than the telephone for taking in large amounts of information. Several banks also allow you to download statements into personal finance management packages. Such ease of access means you stay in control of your finances because you know where you are at all times. Banks are increasingly providing online statements for credit cards as well.

TIP

You can usually pay bills online – all you need are the payee's account details. You can set up a list of payees, then select a payee from the list and enter the amount to be paid.

You can usually pay bills online – all you need are the payees' account details. You can set up a list of payees to save having to type in the details every time you need to pay a bill. You just select a payee from the list and enter the amount to be paid. And the great thing is that you can normally specify the date that you want the bill to be paid, sometimes many months in advance. No more missed credit card payments or angry letters from the gas man. It saves time, effort and postage.

If you make regular payments from your bank account you can set up standing orders and then view, amend or cancel them online. Currently, only a few banks let you set them up online, but this is likely to change as the range of internet banking services widens. Most services will also let you transfer funds electronically between accounts, including accounts held at other banks. This is very useful given that many people have more than one bank account.

You can usually communicate with your bank by e-mail, to order a new cheque book, for example – although it has to be said that not many banks have a good reputation for prompt replies.

The only thing we can't do yet is withdraw cash from our PCs and mobile phones. But even that could change over the next few years with the introduction of smartcards – plastic cards containing a computer chip. Before too long we may be able to slot our smartcards into our PCs and download electronic cash from our bank accounts on to the cards. We could then use them to make small purchases over the internet or in shops that have smartcard readers.

Although banking online does offer a number of advantages, convenience being the main one, it has to be said that telephone banking can do much the same job. And several banks are incorporating mobile phone banking into their fleet of services. So it's not a question of one medium superseding another but of a range of options giving customers the power to bank 'any time, anywhere'.

Some internet banks can offer better-than-average rates on deposits and loans because they don't have expensive branch networks to maintain. Processing transactions over the net is around ten times cheaper than processing them over the phone, and up to a hundred times cheaper than processing them via the bank branch. As well as offering better interest rates, banks may also offer discounts on other products if you apply for them online. They want to encourage you to use the most efficient application method to help them save costs.

After all this enthusiasm, a word of caution. These are still pretty early days for internet banking in the UK. The services are not perfect and many customers have experienced problems with online applications in particular. Many of these problems are easily rectified and are as much to do with the capricious nature of the internet as with the banks themselves. But I know from personal experience that trying and failing to open an account online can be an extremely frustrating experience. Perseverance usually pays off in the end. And the technology will improve as internet banking becomes more popular.

So how do I choose an internet bank?

First of all ask yourself what you want from your bank. Are you simply looking for a high-interest home for your savings, or do you want to carry out a whole range of banking activities as quickly and painlessly as possible? Switching bank accounts can be a hassle – all those direct debits and standing orders to cancel and set up again. Make sure that the bank you choose offers a good range of services and is one that you feel comfortable with. Find out what its security policies are, what steps it takes to keep your details confidential and what it does if the service crashes.

I have my own views on the design and layout of the current crop of banking websites, but you may think differently. Test-drive a few before

> **TIP**
>
> *Make sure that the bank you choose offers a good range of services and is one that you feel comfortable with. Find out what its security policies are, what steps it takes to keep your details confidential and what it does if the service crashes.*

deciding. Many have demonstrations and tours on their websites to help you get a feel for the service. You'll be surprised at how annoying minor design defects can become after you start using a service a lot.

Another point to consider is the speed and reliability of the bank's service, although this is difficult to assess in advance. Just because an internet bank is brand new and state-of-the-art doesn't mean it will necessarily offer the fastest and most reliable service. In fact it's often the new services that experience the most glitches. You've got to ask yourself if you're happy relying entirely on an internet-only, technology-dependent bank or whether you'd prefer one that has an old-fashioned bank branch to walk into if things go wrong.

And don't let all this technological talk blind you to the fact that if a bank is offering you lousy rates of interest on current and savings accounts, onerous overdraft penalties and expensive loans, you shouldn't touch it with a bargepole, no matter how high-tech it is!

Bring on the banks ... and building societies

Many banks' sites work best with certain versions of web browsers. You may need to upgrade your browser to access the bank's services. Most enable you to do this by providing onscreen links to Microsoft or Netscape, the two leading browser manufacturers. The main reason for the upgrade is to ensure that your bank details are protected in transit using the strongest level of encryption currently allowed (128-bit). Also check that your computer is sufficiently powerful to handle the internet banking service. The minimum requirements are detailed on the website. Apple Macintosh users should be particularly alert, as some banks' services don't work with the Mac-OS operating system or Mac-suitable web browsers.

Bank of Scotland (www.bankofscotland.co.uk)

The Bank of Scotland pioneered PC banking in the UK with its Home and Office Banking System (HOBS), initially a direct-dial service. It has now added an internet banking service called **INTERNET HOBS** (www.internethobs.co.uk) and offers its own free internet access for customers. You have to open an account before you can set up internet banking, however.

The site is fun and approachable, although the demo requires you to download Macromedia Shockwave software if you haven't already got it. There's a good range of services on offer plus the knowledge that you're plugged into a bank

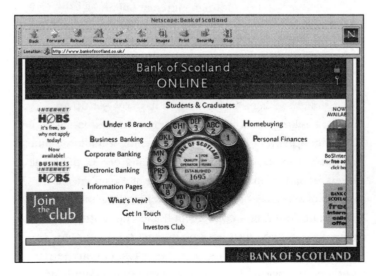

The Bank of Scotland's site is fun and approachable and has a good range of services.

with many years' experience of electronic banking, a good reputation, as well as an extensive branch and cash machine network.

Type of service	PC and internet
Cost	Free
Hours	6am–1am
Accounts covered	All
View transactions	Up to 30 business days
Bill payments	Available from summer 2000
Standing orders/	
Direct debits	View, amend, delete
Transfer funds	
a) internally	Yes
b) externally	No
Credit card balances	Last 30 working days
Misc.	You can order travellers' cheques and foreign currency online

Barclays Bank (www.ibank.barclays.co.uk)

Barclays was one of the first to launch direct-dial banking, but many commentators thought it had missed a trick by not going straight to internet banking. It has now set up an internet banking service and is reaping the rewards – it is the UK's largest internet bank with approaching a million online customers. It is widely recognized as being one of the leading players in online financial services. The site combines a number of other services, such as stockbroking and Barclaycard, offering a convenient 'joined up' approach to online finance. You also get free internet access for life. This has got to be the future, and Barclays is heading in the right direction. The site is sophisticated, well designed and easy to use. If you're not already a Barclays customer, you can apply online. If you like the idea of all your financial services easily to hand in one place, this is an excellent service.

*The Barclays site is sophisticated and easy to use. It combines
online banking with a number of other services, such as stockbroking
and Barclaycard.*

Type of service	Internet
Cost	Free
Hours	24-hour
Accounts covered	Personal and business, current, deposit and loan
View transactions	Last six weeks
Bill payments	Two years in advance
Standing orders/ Direct debits	View, amend, delete
Transfer funds a) internally	Yes
b) externally	Yes
Credit card balances	Last six months
Misc.	You can download statements into personal finance software programs, such as Microsoft Money, and into Excel spreadsheets.

23

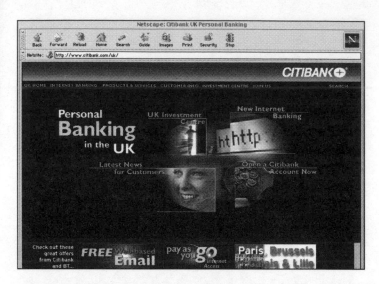

Citibank offers customers accounts in different currencies; particularly useful for business travellers and people who work abroad.

Citibank (www.citibank.co.uk)

Citibank is one of the pioneers of PC banking in the USA, but it has only three branches in the UK. It relies on agreements with other banks to offer the full range of banking facilities. For example, you can deposit cheques in branches of Lloyds TSB as long as they're for £1,000 or less. Otherwise you have to send them by post, which is fine so long as they don't get lost. Withdrawing cash is no problem as you can use most high-street cash machines.

Citibank is notable for its emphasis on international banking, offering its customers accounts in different currencies, such as dollars and Euros. This is particularly useful for business travellers and people who work abroad. It was also one of the first banks to offer funds transfers to other bank accounts. The bank's service was legitimately criticized for slow download times thanks to a misconfiguration of its computer systems. They've now introduced more capacity to handle the traffic flow and the service has thankfully speeded up. The internet banking service is supplemented by telephone banking.

Type of service	Internet
Cost	Free
Hours	24-hour
Accounts covered	Current, deposit
View transactions	Last 90 days
Bill payments	Up to four months in advance
Standing orders	Set up, amend, cancel
Transfer funds	
a) internally:	Yes
b) externally:	Yes (can set up online and also transfer to Citibank customers abroad)
Credit card balances	No
Misc.	You can order travellers' cheques online in a range of currencies, including sterling, dollars, deutschmarks and yen.

The Co-operative Bank (www.co-operativebank.co.uk)

The Co-operative Bank was one of the early adopters of internet banking. In fact, it is so enthusiastic about the whole concept of online financial services that it has established an internet-only bank, called Smile (*see below*). This shouldn't detract from its own internet service which is admirably simple and straightforward, with a neat design and an uncluttered feel. Such simplicity of design helps keep download times as short as possible. It's just a shame you have to resort to the phone to set up funds transfers and bill payments, but this is likely to change before too long.

The Co-operative Bank's site is simple and straightforward, keeping download times as short as possible.

Type of service	Internet
Cost	Free
Hours	24-hour
Accounts covered	Current, savings, credit card, personal loan
View transactions	Last six months
Bill payments	Have to set up payee list by phone first, thereafter can pay online, but can't specify future date.
Standing orders	Set up, amend, cancel
Direct debits	View, delete
Transfer funds	
a) internally	Have to set up by phone first
b) externally	Ditto
Credit card balances	Last four months
Misc.	You can order cheque books and paying books online, as well as copies of statements.

Egg (www.egg.co.uk)

Egg, the internet banking arm of insurance giant Prudential, made a name for itself with a savings account that was so popular Egg had to make it internet-only to stem the demand in the end. It has since added mortgages, personal loans and credit cards to its online offerings and is promising a full range of banking and investment services before too long. Its partial stock market flotation should help it raise funds for further expansion and refinements of its service.

Egg has not been without its problems, however. Its internet-only status put a lot of strain on untested technology and it experienced tremendous technical difficulties with the launch of its internet-only credit card, for example. But it claims to have eliminated most of the gremlins by now. What Egg has done very successfully is to show that, with strong backing and management commitment, an entirely new brand can be established on the web very quickly

Egg is an internet-only bank offering savings accounts, mortgages, personal loans and credit cards.

offering competitive products. The site design is hip, if a little annoying when it allows aesthetics to get in the way of logic. Online application forms have been improved to make them faster to complete.

Type of service	Internet
Cost	Free
Hours	24-hour
Accounts covered	Savings, credit cards, loans, mortgages
View transactions	Last five transactions
Bill payments	Egg credit card, monthly direct debit
Standing orders	N/A
Direct debits	Egg credit card
Transfer funds	
a) internally	Yes
b) externally	Only to accounts in your name
Credit card balances	Last five transactions
Misc.	Egg also offers online shopping from its site with a 2% discount if you use its credit card.

First Direct (www.firstdirect.co.uk)

First Direct, the pioneer of branchless telephone banking owned by HSBC, was also relatively early to offer PC banking. But it stuck with direct-dial banking for a surprisingly long time, only rolling out a full internet service in February 2000. The direct-dial banking interface was based on the Internet Explorer web browser to help ease the transition when it eventually offered net banking. But unlike Barclays, First Direct is allowing customers to stick with direct-dial banking if they want to, acknowledging that some people feel more comfortable with this type of service. The bank also plans to offer WAP mobile phone banking from July 2000 in a deal with BT Cellnet, and digital TV banking on Sky's Open platform from October 2000.

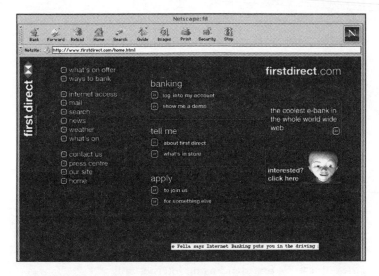

The First Direct site offers easy access to all accounts and transaction histories.

The site is notable for its simplicity and the clarity of its design, which offers easy access to all accounts and transaction histories. Again, it's a shame bill payments have to be set up over the telephone first – this negates some of the advantages of online banking – but overall the service is well-designed and conceived. Customers also have the added security of a fully fledged telephone banking back-up and ease of access to all HSBC branches.

Type of service	Direct-dial and internet
Cost	Free
Hours	24-hour
Accounts covered	Current, savings, credit card, loan, Individual Savings Account
View transactions	Last three months
Bill payments	Up to a year in advance (telephone set up)
Standing orders	View

Direct debits	View
Transfer funds	
a) internally	Yes
b) externally	Yes
Credit card balances	Last two months
Misc.	You can download account information into personal finance management packages, order foreign currency online, and apply for free mobile phone banking so long as you have a BT Cellnet phone.

First-e (www.first-e.com)

First-e, the UK's first stand-alone internet-only
bank, is a joint venture between Irish technology
company Enba Systems and French private bank Banque
d'Escompte. It started off as a high-interest savings bank

*First-e started life as a high-interest savings bank. It is adding a current
account and a sharedealing account to its services.*

offering the best savings rates around. It is adding a current account and sharedealing account that includes the facility to invest in companies floating on the stock market for the first time. As First-e is an offshore bank the interest is paid without tax deducted (gross) and you have to declare the amount of gross interest earned on your annual tax return. It has the edge on Egg in that interest is paid monthly rather than yearly, giving customers the benefit of compounding.

Although you can open a deposit account in minutes online and transfer money to it, the account isn't fully authorized until you've proved your identity with various documents, such as a copy of your driving licence. First-e doesn't process cash or cheques, so deposits have to be made electronically, or if you have kept an account with another bank you can phone them and ask them to do it.

The service hasn't escaped the technical hitches bedevilling many new internet ventures – the online application process is still not glitch-free. The system requires the latest versions of browsers and for them to be able to read Java applets – small programs written in a computer language devised by Sun Microsystems, a software company. This has led to confusion amongst prospective customers. Assuming First-e can sort all these problems out, its banking service is certainly attractive for its competitive rates. And if it can keep overheads to a minimum, a whole range of attractively priced products should be coming our way. It's well worth a look if you can put up with the occasional technical frustration.

Those worried about the bank's French regulatory status should bear in mind that complaints ultimately have to be made to the Banque de France, but that the country's Deposit Guarantee Fund compensates customers up to Euros 70,000 (around £45,000).

Type of service	Internet
Cost	Free
Hours	24-hour
Accounts covered	Current, savings (share dealing planned)
View transactions	Complete history
Bill payments	No limit
Standing orders	N/A
Direct debits	N/A
Transfer funds	
a) internally	Yes
b) externally	Yes
Credit card balances	N/A
Misc.	Encrypted statements sent by e-mail.

Halifax (www.halifax-online.co.uk)

Halifax has made bold moves on to the internet recently, setting up internet banking and sharedealing services, plus a £750 million investment in a new stand-alone bank called **Intelligent Finance** (www.if.com). In February 2000 it also announced a link up with BT Cellnet, the mobile phone network operator, to offer banking via internet-enabled mobile phones (Wireless Application Protocol, or WAP phones).

Although Halifax's site is admirably simple, I feel they overdo it to the extent that the service appears a little simplistic. As with several other internet banks, you have to set up standing orders and bill payments by telephone first, which seems to defeat the object. The site gives the impression that it has only gone halfway to realizing all that the internet can offer the customer in terms of functionality – there's little cross-reference to other Halifax financial services, for example. But at least it won't overawe the internet ingénue.

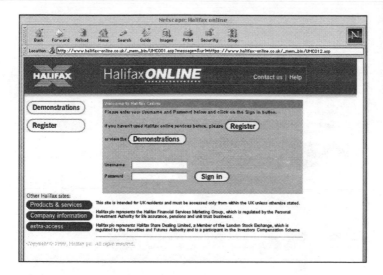

Halifax has internet banking and sharedealing services and is now setting up banking services via internet-enabled mobile phones.

Type of service	Internet
Cost	Free
Hours	24-hour
Accounts covered	Current
View transactions	Last 60 transactions
Bill payments	Yes, but can't specify future date
Standing orders	View, cancel
Direct debits	View, cancel
Transfer funds	
a) internally	Yes
b) externally	Yes
Credit card balances	N/A

Lloyds TSB (www.lloydstsb.com)

Lloyds TSB was rather late to the internet and there is a danger that it is being left behind by nimbler and more forward-thinking rivals. Banking behemoths

The Lloyds TSB site is stylish and well laid out.

seldom move quickly, yet the pace of change on the
net is punishing. Lloyds' existing service is stylish
nonetheless and well laid out, but still feels a little basic,
with online set-up facilities rather limited. Transfers to
external bank accounts and bill payments have to be
pre-arranged. You get the feeling that this is a bank that
has introduced an online service because it had to, not
because it wanted to.

Type of service	Internet
Cost	Free
Hours	4am until midnight
Accounts covered	All
View transactions	Up to two months
Bill payments	Up to a year in advance (have to set up by phone)
Standing orders	View, amend, cancel
Direct debits	View

Transfer funds
   a) internally   Yes
   b) externally   Yes
Credit card balances   N/A
Misc.   You can download statements into
                      personal finance management
                      programs or as a simple text file.
                      There's also a feature that checks
                      your browser version to test whether
                      it is compatible with the service.

Marbles (www.marbles.com)

The first thing to be said about HFC's online credit card is
that it has nothing to do with Marbles, the public relations
company (**www.marbles.co.uk**), which is understandably
miffed at the confusion given that it bagged the name first.
You would have thought HFC could have thought of another
suitably silly name, but there we are, that's the net for you.
Anyway, Marbles is one of those low-APR cards introduced to
the UK by aggressive US card companies. HFC promises a
decision on your online application within 60 seconds,
although the complete application process takes a lot longer
because of the necessity for a written signature on the
contract. You can transfer balances from other cards to
Marbles online and interrogate your account 24 hours a day.
There's also an internet shopping guarantee whereby Marbles
guarantees that you won't be liable for any fraudulent use of
your card, providing you haven't been negligent with it. In
reality, this guarantee is a bit of a marketing gimmick given
that most card providers won't hold you liable for so called
'card not present' fraud.

Type of service   Internet
Cost   Free

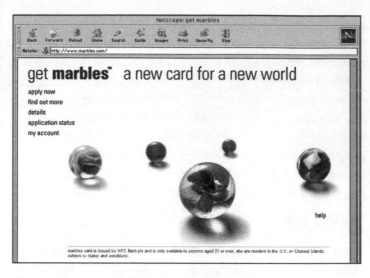

Marbles offers a low-APR credit card for which you can apply online.

Hours	24-hour
Accounts covered	Credit card only
View transactions	Last three months
Bill payments	N/A
Standing orders	N/A
Direct debits	N/A
Transfer funds	
a) internally	N/A
b) externally	N/A
Credit card balances	As above
Misc.	You can change your statement date online.

Nationwide Building Society (www.nationwide.co.uk)

The Nationwide Building Society pioneered internet banking in the UK, offering free internet access, and a range of football information services thanks to its sponsorship of the Football League. It found itself becoming a destination site in its own right, regardless of the banking services it could offer. Nationwide was one of the first financial institutions to make its website more interactive. For example, they now include animated sequences on the site and online applications for a range of products. And it is one of the few internet services that will allow you to set up standing orders online without having to phone first. The differences may be slight at first glance, but Nationwide just goes that one step further than other internet banks, making for a more rounded, fully functional service. Hats off to them.

Type of service	Internet
Cost	Free
Hours	24-hour
Accounts covered	FlexAccount, card-based savings accounts
View transactions	Up to 90 days
Bill payments	Up to a month in advance

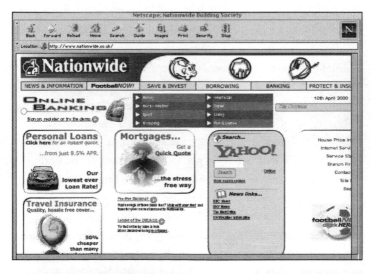

The Nationwide Building Society pioneered internet banking in the UK and was one of the first to make its site more interactive.

Standing orders	Set up, amend, cancel
Direct debits	View
Transfer funds	
a) internally	Yes
b) externally	Yes (including abroad)
Credit card balances	N/A
Misc.	You can apply for a new PIN or a reminder if you've forgotten your old one, and carry out a number of other housekeeping tasks online, including ordering stationery. There's also an online quotation facility for personal loans and a useful message manager for sending and receiving encrypted e-mails.

Norwich & Peterborough Building Society

(www.npbs.co.uk)

Norwich & Peterborough Building Society has been one of the few building societies to cotton on to the internet's potential to reach a wider audience than their locality would normally dictate. The internet is not constrained by geography. It is surprising that more building societies, usually serving particular areas of the country, are not rushing online in an effort to appeal to the nation as a whole. Norwich & Peterborough's Netmaster account is admirably clear and well laid out. You get to see all the information you're most likely to need without wasting time having to click through several pages. But the breadth of service is somewhat limited, with standing orders, bill payments and external transfers having to be set up by telephone first. And the inability to transfer funds externally to other bank accounts is virtually inexplicable. Let's hope Norwich & Peterborough amends this soon.

The Norwich & Peterborough Building Society is using its online services to extend the geographic distribution of its customer pool.

Type of service	Internet
Cost	Free for Gold Current Account holders. After first six months Business Gold account holders charged £7.99 per month.
Hours	24-hour
Accounts covered	Current, savings
View transactions	Last six months
Bill payments	Up to two years in advance
Standing orders	View, amend, cancel (set up by phone first)
Direct debits:	View, cancel
Transfer funds	
a) internally	Yes
b) externally	No
Credit card balances	N/A

Royal Bank of Scotland (www.rbs.co.uk)

Royal Bank of Scotland (RBS) was another of the pioneers in the internet banking field, launching its service back in 1997. It has since upgraded the level of functionality to make it one of the most sophisticated of the internet banking services around. You can set up standing orders, bill payments and fund transfers online, putting it well ahead of many competitors. The screens are well designed, but it's the degree of functionality that really stands out. The services come close to realizing the true potential of the internet – giving customers total control of their finances. RBS recently took control of NatWest so thankfully all those long suffering NatWest customers who've been lumbered with direct-dial banking are now being given internet banking.

Type of service   Internet

Cost   Free

The Royal Bank of Scotland's site is one of the most sophisticated of the internet banking services.

Hours	24-hour
Accounts covered	Current, savings, ISAs, loans
View transactions	Last six months
Bill payments	Up to 120 days in advance
Standing orders	Set up, view, amend, cancel
Direct debits	View, cancel
Transfer funds	
a) internally	Yes
b) externally	Yes (can set up online)
Credit card balances	N/A
Misc.	You can order cheque books and paying-in books online, as well as download statement information into personal finance packages or spreadsheets.

Smile (www.smile.co.uk)

Yes it's one of these stand-alone internet-only banks with a silly name. Although it is owned by the Co-operative Bank, it is entirely separate from its parent, much as First Direct is separate from HSBC. But it is a full banking service, offering current accounts with a cheque book and card. You can apply for an account online – savings or current, although you get a better rate of interest on your savings if you're a current account holder. The site is very smart, with good use of colour and graphics and it has obviously been well executed. As it is internet-only, interest rates on current account credit balances and savings are above average. It makes big play of security and even encrypts e-mails to and from customers. The only criticism I have is the inability to specify a future date for bill payments.

Type of service	Internet
Cost	Free

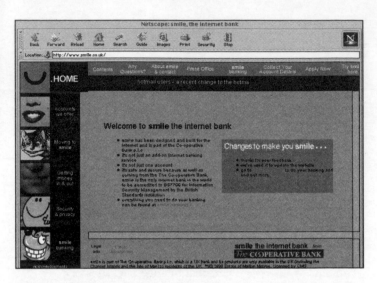

Smile is an internet-only bank that offers above-average interest rates on its savings and current accounts. It places great emphasis on security.

Hours	24-hour
Accounts covered	All
View transactions	Last four months
Bill payments	Can't set up online, can't specify payment date
Standing orders	Set up, view, amend, cancel
Direct debits	View, cancel
Transfer funds	
a) internally	Yes
b) externally	Yes
Credit card balances	Last four months
Misc.	The 'Customer Services' section includes an impressive array of facilities, including requesting overdraft or credit-limit increases, replacement cards, foreign currency and so on.

Woolwich (www.woolwich.co.uk)

Woolwich has been very brave in its internet planning. It has devised Open Plan Services, an ambitious scheme to allow customers to access a whole range of products in any way they wish, whether that's via a branch, computer, hand-held organizer or mobile phone. The idea is to bring all products together into one place to give customers control over all their finances. The internet banking section enables customers to view statements for all their Woolwich products on one screen. It's all very high-tech and impressively designed and

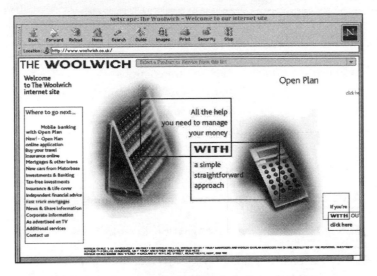

Woolwich has devised an ambitious all-inclusive scheme that allows customers to access a whole range of products via a branch, computer, hand-held organizer or mobile phone.

Woolwich should be applauded for its boldness. Whether customers are ready for such an all-inclusive approach remains to be seen, but Woolwich is undoubtedly moving in the direction that other banks will inevitably have to follow. Having said all this, it comes as a bit of a disappointment to find out that bill payments and standing orders still have to be set up by phone first. Two steps forward, one step back!

Type of service	Internet
Cost	Free
Hours	24-hour
Accounts covered	All banking products
View transactions	Last 100 transactions
Bill payments	Up to six weeks in advance (set up by telephone first)
Standing orders	View (set up by telephone first)
Direct debits	View
Transfer funds	
a) internally	Yes
b) externally	Yes
Credit card balances	Last 100 transactions
Misc.	Internet-enabled mobile phone banking is being rolled out at the moment. It will duplicate all internet banking facilities.

And coming soon ...

Abbey National (www.abbeynational.co.uk)

Abbey National is making up for lost time by joining the internet revolution in a big way. It launched its own internet service in April 2000 as an added channel for its existing branch-based network. It promises full interactivity, including the ability to set up bill payments and standing orders online.

It is also launching a totally separate internet-only bank called Cahoot, due for launch in July. Customers will be able to access its services via digital television (satellite and cable), WAP phones and the internet. The stand-alone bank intends to target and reward the most profitable customers, offering

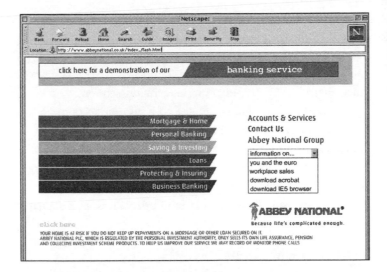

Abbey National is launching a fully-interactive internet service to complement its existing branch-based network.

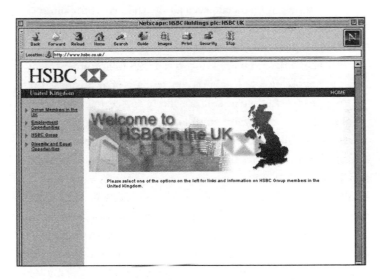

HSBC's internet banking service is likely to be launched in late 2000.

them improved deals based on their usage. It also wants to make the website a destination in its own right, forming partnerships with holiday companies, such as Thomas Cook, and retailers, such as Blackstar, the online DVD specialist and video retailer, and Dell, the computer manufacturer.

Banking services will be limited to a current account and a credit card to start with, but savings accounts will follow. Customers won't be allowed to use the Abbey National branch network, but they will have access to its cash machine network. We're likely to see credit-card customers offered discounts for using their cards at partner retailers, in a similar fashion to the Egg model.

HSBC (www.hsbc.co.uk)

HSBC, which owns First Direct, has now rebranded all its Midland Bank branches with the HSBC logo. The lack of any internet banking service from Midland has been one of the great mysteries in financial services. It has settled for direct-dial banking and has concentrated on digital TV banking, via Sky's Open platform, for example.

But HSBC has now announced a £1.25 billion investment strategy involving wholesale moves of its global business on to the internet. But we're still not likely to see internet banking for UK customers until late 2000. WAP mobile phone banking isn't likely to be introduced until the following year.

Chapter 3

Investing

Introduction

Sharedealing over the internet, or trading online to use the US phrase, has been the most dynamic and exciting area of financial services in 1999–2000. The net is fantastic at handling large amounts of data, making it easily accessible and visually attractive. It is also perfectly suited to online dealing, where the ability to transact in seconds is paramount.

For the first time ordinary investors have had the same resources as professional investors in the City. In the old days, information was power. If you were first with the news you could act on it before others and make money. The private investor was usually several steps behind the professionals, buying or selling too late.

But the internet has revolutionized the whole investing world. These days private investors can buy and sell instantaneously, get up-to-the-second portfolio valuations, read stock market and company news, and bury their noses in tons of research freely available online. Even major international stockbrokers that would normally charge their institutional clients large sums for company research and buy or sell recommendations are giving it away free to private investors.

Eventually investment information will become a commodity and investors will be able to find out anything they want online. But there's some way to go before we reach that situation, so some online stockbrokers can still get the edge on their competitors by offering superior research facilities.

What's more, dealing online is generally cheaper than dealing over the phone because there are no expensive human beings involved – just expensive computer systems. And the great thing about computer systems is that they can handle significantly more traffic without the need for a proportionate increase in computing power. So the more people that deal online, the lower commissions should become – in theory.

Online sharedealing takes off

Making something easier for people to do tends to make them do it more often. And this is nowhere more obvious than in the field of online dealing. Brokers have been overwhelmed by the level of demand from eager investors clamouring to jump on board the investment bandwagon. This demand has largely been fuelled by a fascination with technology stocks. Some brokers' telephone dealing operations have been strained to breaking point, which is why they're so keen to push people on to the net. Anything that automates the process has got to be good news for their operations.

According to the Association of Private Client Investment Managers and Stockbrokers (APCIMS), the UK industry's main trade body, the number of online trading accounts more than

doubled in the last three months of 1999 to over 100,000.
APCIMS fully expects the figure to double and maybe treble
by the end of 2000. Investment bank JP Morgan estimates that
there will be around 2 million UK online investors by 2002.
In Europe as a whole, Forrester Research thinks there will be
14 million online brokerage accounts by 2004.

That's a phenomenal rate of growth. It explains why so
many new online brokers are entering the fray and why
dealing commissions are also beginning to fall thanks to
increased competition. US brokers in particular have
aggressively entered the UK market, but now continental
European brokers are also setting up shop here. At the end of
1998 there were just two brokers offering online dealing in
the UK. At the last count there were approaching 20. Those
brokers that have established a presence are experiencing an
explosive growth in demand and are also finding that internet
customers deal five to seven times more often than their
telephone customers.

What is online trading ?

Although buying and selling shares is the most popular
investment activity online, you can also invest in
individual savings accounts, futures and options, and foreign
currency. Soon we will be able to invest online in any
number of unit trusts and investment funds, too. At this early
stage, however, this guide will focus on buying shares and
investment funds online.

As with online banking there's an important distinction to
be made between types of online dealing service. Some just
offer e-mail trading. This means that you send your 'buy' or
'sell' order by e-mail from the website and a broker carries it
out for you in person. But the real McCoy is 'real-time'

dealing, where your order is processed immediately without any human intervention. As this is an internet guide, we will concentrate on 'real-time dealing' as the best kind of service for investors.

Sending e-mail orders is not much different to dealing over the phone. And the problem is that you don't actually know the price at which you will buy the shares because of the inevitable time delay between your order being sent and it being received, understood and executed. It may only be a matter of minutes, but share prices can move significantly in that time. Brokers that only offer e-mail ordering also tend not to be very sophisticated in other areas of service. And there's a greater chance of error when fallible humans are involved.

You're the boss!

Another point to make is that most online brokers are execution-only – that is, they don't offer any advice based on your individual circumstances. They may well include their own views on the general state of the markets and even give some share tips, but such advice is for all their customers and not just you. The theory is that the type of investor who is happy to trade online is usually savvy enough to do his or her own research, too. But some brokers do offer advice, with the extra cost being incorporated into the dealing commission, or charge separately on an *ad hoc* basis. Check out what kind of service the broker offers before you open an account.

In the USA, brokers are trying to develop sophisticated online stock and fund selection tools that will help investors choose the right investments. For example, the investor may fill in a questionnaire asking about their age, financial situation and tolerance of risk. The broker's automated system will then throw up some shares or funds it deems suitable. In the UK we're some way away from that level of service. So if you're keen on the stock market, but you're unsure how to choose companies or funds to invest in, you should seek independent financial advice, or use an online broker who does offer advice, before taking the plunge.

So how do I choose an internet stockbroker?

First you've got to decide what kind of investor you are or intend to be. Ask yourself the following questions, then match your answers against our reviews of the brokers in this chapter to find the one that best suits your needs.

> **TIP**
>
> *If you're keen on the stock market, but unsure how to choose companies or funds to invest in, seek independent financial advice or use an online broker who offers advice.*

- Are you just dipping your toe gingerly into the water, or do you fancy yourself as a real wheeler-dealer trading almost daily?

- Do you have a few thousand to invest, or tens of thousands?

- Do you want to play safe or take big risks in the hope of hitting the jackpot?

- Are you confident that you can do your own research, or do you think you'll need advice at some stage?

- Do you want as much research information as possible at your disposal on your broker's site, or are you happy to find it elsewhere?

- Do you want the option to deal in other ways – via the telephone, mobile phone or hand-held computer, for example?

- Are you happy just dealing in shares, or do you want the option to invest in investment funds, such as unit trusts, and other investments, such as futures, options and foreign currency?

- Are you happy sticking to the UK market or do you want to seek investment opportunities on stock exchanges around the world?

- Would you mind if your investments were held electronically in a nominee account on your behalf and you didn't receive share certificates? (With a nominee account your name doesn't go on the share register but you retain the benefit of the shares and your entitlement to company reports and any shareholder perks.)

- How important is the level of dealing commission to you?

Most of the internet brokers have demos on their sites. Check them out. It's important to get the feel of a service before you sign up. The site may be very sophisticated but poorly designed, or simply not your style. And how much online help do they provide? Some of the information websites mentioned below also provide useful guides to choosing a broker.

How does online dealing actually work?

First you have to open an account. Some brokers allow you to do this online straight away, others require proof of identity documentation, which means it can take up to two weeks to open the account. After that you're usually issued with a user name and password or personal identification number (PIN). This is to prevent anyone going online and buying shares in your name without your authority. Keeping your security details secret is your responsibility. If you lose or forget your password/PIN, most brokers will send it to you by e-mail so long as you can answer another pre-agreed security question.

You normally have to open the account with an initial deposit – some brokers impose a minimum. You can send this by cheque or make a direct transfer from your bank account. Electronic

> **TIP**
>
> *Most internet brokers have demos on their sites. Check them out. It's important to get the feel of a service before you sign up.*

transfer is the easiest. Once you've set up a variable direct debit you can then transfer funds back and forth between your bank and sharedealing accounts very easily.

After that, away you go. Do some research into the companies you're thinking of investing in, using the broker's own research tools and external ones as necessary. When you're ready to trade, you normally go through to the trading section, enter the stock market code of the company you want to buy or sell (there's usually a 'look-up' facility if you don't know it) and then enter the number of shares or the amount you want to invest.

The best brokers will then give you a live price quote that you can either accept or reject. If you like the price, press enter. Most brokers also give you the opportunity to place a 'limit order' where you can specify the price you want to deal at. Normally this is on a 'fill or kill' basis, which means that the deal is cancelled immediately if it can't be completed at the price you want. Some brokers will keep limit orders open until the end of the trading day. This facility also means you can place orders out of market hours – at the weekend, say.

When you've entered your order, you're then normally given a last chance to review it and make sure you haven't made a mistake. Check over the details carefully – there's no going back after this point. If you're happy, press the submit button. Your order is then processed instantaneously (unless there is some reason why it has to be completed manually by the broker – if it is outside normal market size, for example). You're then quoted a unique order number to prove that the transaction was made and executed and sent an electronic contract note recording the terms on which the deal was made. It's a good idea to print these off.

Your orders are scrambled using 128-bit encryption so it's virtually impossible for anyone to intercept confidential information as it is sent across the web. Brokers also have sophisticated 'firewall' security protecting their computer systems from unauthorized infiltration.

WARNING

Sharedealing on the net is very fast and easy to do. It can also become addictive if you're not careful. So make sure you know what you're doing before you speculate away your life savings. You shouldn't invest more than you can afford to lose. Investments can go down as well as up... etc... etc....

Information is power

Before we get to the brokers themselves, you should add a few choice investment information websites to your web browser's 'Favorites' or 'Bookmarks' folder. No broker offers everything you need yet, although some come close.

There are so many useful resources online that there isn't space in this guide to mention them all. Here's some of the best from the current crop.

Citywire (www.citywire.co.uk)

A neat, well focused site providing company and stock market news packaged for the private investor. Citywire aims to trump rival financial news service AFX by offering analysis and comment as well as the facts. It also provides company data, news of secret share purchases and sales, and sections on investment funds, too. They don't go a bundle on flashy design, but then that helps achieve fast download times.

Citywire is a financial news service that provides company data and news as well as analysis and comment.

European Investor (www.europeaninvestor.com)

European Investor is a truly excellent site for investors with a global outlook. Cross-border trading will become far more common when more UK brokers offer such services. In the meantime there are European brokers that will accept UK customers. You can often get cheaper dealing and greater access to global markets. This site helps you find them. European Investor provides data from most of the world's markets, albeit with an emphasis on Europe. It has also introduced a system that rates brokers according to a number of criteria, such as the facility to deal globally and dealing costs. When you consider that there are over 700 online brokers in Europe, this is obviously an extremely useful resource. There are European-focused share tips, and information on initial public offerings across the continent, plus news from various services, such as Reuters, AFX, PR Newswire and Business Wire. This site goes from strength to strength.

FreeQuotes (www.freequotes.co.uk)

As its name suggests, this site provides free share prices for investors. But unlike many other sites, the prices are real-time, not delayed. There's also access to company news, portfolio monitoring and the facility to set up alerts. This means FreeQuotes will let you know by e-mail when certain share prices reach a level you've specified. The site is simple and unpretentious and particularly useful if your broker charges you for live prices on your portfolio.

FT.com (www.ft.com)

The *Financial Times* online newspaper has been completely revamped in a bid to become the world's leading provider of

European Investor helps you find European brokers that offer UK customers cheaper dealing and greater access to global markets.

FreeQuotes provides free real-time share prices as well as company news and portfolio monitoring.

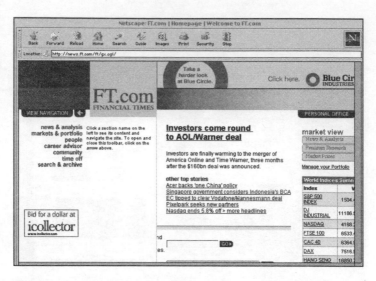

If you are serious about the world of sharedealing and investment, you should visit the FT.com site for some top class comment and analysis.

business and financial data. The breadth of information available is extremely impressive, covering most of the world's major markets and economies. The quality of comment and analysis is also top class. Plus there are new discussion groups and shopping facilities on the site, to make it more fun and interactive. If you're serious about investing, FT.com is a must.

Hemmington Scott (www.hemscott.net)

Hemmington Scott has transformed itself from a rather dowdy publisher into one of the leading online financial information providers. Its new service, Hemscott.net Business, packages company financial results, business news, broker consensus forecasts and share price information. You can also find out details of directors' sharedealings. It is a very powerful and well designed resource. The only catch is that if

Hemscott.net Business packages financial results, business news, forecasts and price information in a powerful and well designed website.

you want free access to all of this you have to have Hemscott as your internet service provider (ISP). It's free and it doesn't mean you have to get rid of any existing ISP accounts you have. If you can't, or don't want to have hemscott.net as your ISP, a subscription to Business Plus costs £10 plus VAT a month.

Interactive Investor International (III) (www.iii.co.uk)

Interactive Investor has been aggressively developing its site into a general personal finance portal, with links to product providers as well as guides and financial news. Its recent flotation has given it cash to expand further. But it started out as a pure investment site and it is still an excellent resource in this respect. You can track your investment portfolio, see what it's worth and how much profit you've made, and look at company share price graphs. III also has a thriving

The Interactive Investor International site has an excellent tool to help you choose an internet broker.

community of private investors posting opinions, news and gossip on company-specific bulletin boards.

There's also an excellent tool to help you choose an internet broker, including a table that compares their main features and a commission calculator. You simply enter how much you're going to invest and up pops the broker with the cheapest commission for that deal. The complicated tariff structures employed by most brokers means that you tend to get a different 'best buy' for different deal sizes. But if you know roughly how much you're likely to invest each time, the calculator is useful for finding a broker that's good value for that size of deal. Of course, there's more to choosing a broker than the commission level, as we've seen above. III is in the processing of adding links through to the brokers so that investors can open an account more easily, using III as the gateway.

London Stock Exchange (www.londonstockexchange.co.uk)

The LSE's official site contains lots of useful background information for private investors, as well as share prices and details of the companies listed in its new technology sector techMARK. There's information on the Alternative Investment Market – the smaller, less tightly regulated market for fledgling companies – and simple guides and glossaries.

For useful background information of companies listed in the AIM, check out the London Stock Exchange site.

Market-Eye (www.market-eye.co.uk)

Market-Eye is the private investor service from information provider Primark Datastream/ICV. The look of the site makes it resemble a professional dealing screen used by City dealers – differently coloured figures on a black screen. The service is divided according to the level of sophistication that you need. At the most basic level, anyone can access delayed

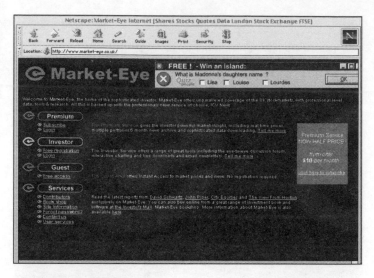

Market-Eye has different levels of information services, catering for the simply curious to the serious investor.

share prices and stock market index figures without having to register. If you do register, you get free access to more information, such as company performance data and graphing facilities. There's also a bulletin board or chat forum (they're given various names on different websites), analysis from guest columnists and an investment-related bookshop. There are also links to several internet stockbrokers on the site.

Serious investors who trade frequently can pay £10 a month for an even more sophisticated 'Premium' level of service. You can choose a combination of delayed and real-time prices to suit you, an expanded news service including historical company announcements, economic news and market reports. Five-year historical company performance data can also be downloaded in a variety of file formats to suit most home finance packages. Premium service customers

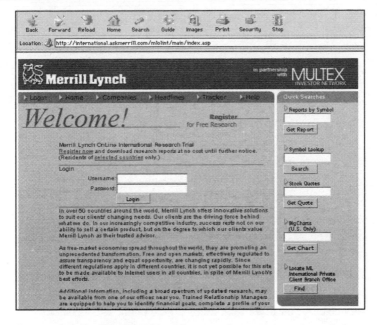

By registering for Merrill Lynch's trial you can have access to research that would normally be reserved for paying professionals.

can also receive daily portfolio valuations by e-mail. All in all, Market-Eye offers what most investors need, from the novice to the expert.

Merrill Lynch (http://international.askmerrill.com)

Merrill Lynch is the largest stockbroker in the world and even a company of its size is experimenting with giving away its research to private investors for free. If you're looking for detailed, knowledgeable reports about companies both sides of the Atlantic, register for Merrill's trial. This is research that would normally be reserved for paying professionals. Private investors have never had such access before and it is giving them unprecedented control and power.

MoneyWorld (www.moneyworld.co.uk)

This is the granddaddy of all finance internet sites, now owned by Exchange Holdings, which also owns Moneyextra. The two finance brands are gradually merging and the MoneyWorld name will probably be subsumed into Moneyextra. It is an excellent personal finance portal with a comprehensive investments section. There's plenty of useful information, including ISA guides, a portfolio management service, investor bulletin boards for news and comment, share prices and graphs, and easy fund performance comparisons. There are plenty of links through to product providers, too. If you're looking for an internet broker, MoneyWorld also details all their commission rates for various deal sizes. Its definition of what constitutes online dealing is a little looser than this guide's, including e-mail services, but all in all this site is an excellent and versatile resource for investment newcomers.

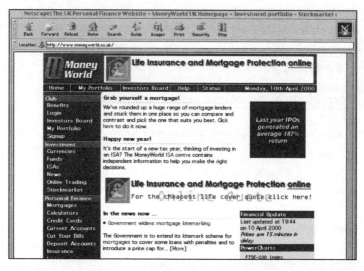

The MoneyWorld site is an excellent resource for novices.

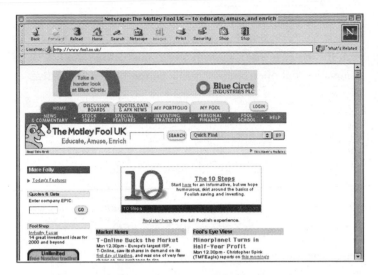

Motley Fool UK is an upbeat site packed full of useful information.

Motley Fool UK (www.fool.co.uk)

The Motley Fool is a US-based website known for
its irreverent and lighthearted approach to the whole
business of investment. Its UK site follows much the same
style, but that's not to say they're frivolous – far from it.
There's plenty of valuable information on how to invest,
how to choose a broker (including a comprehensive
breakdown of commissions for various sizes of deal),
plus the usual companies and markets news. It is also
extending its informal approach to other areas of finance.
This is a site designed by investors for investors and comes
highly recommended.

Ofex (www.ofex.co.uk)

Ofex is the unregulated market for very small companies run
by market maker JP Jenkins. As yet you can't invest online in

Ofex-listed companies, you have to deal by phone. But interest has been growing in the market as wily investors look for the next major growth stock. Successful Ofex companies will often seek a listing on the bigger Alternative Investment Market or the main market, so speculative investors try to spot them when they're still tiny, in the hope of making a spectacular return later. The site lists share prices and company financial results. If interest continues to rise, Ofex should become more automated, enabling its information to be shown on broker and investment information websites. But speculators are unlikely to be able to invest online in Ofex stocks for some time.

TrustNet (www.trustnet.co.uk)

TrustNet started off as a site tightly focused on UK investment trusts, providing price, performance and portfolio data for each trust. It has since expanded the service to include all investment funds, including unit trusts and open-ended investment companies (OEICS).

UK-iNvest.com (www.uk-invest.com)

UK-iNvest provides investment content for Freeserve, the UK's largest free internet service provider, but the site is also accessible at its own address. Owned by GlobalNet Financial, a US information provider that is currently launching similar websites across the world, UK-iNvest is simply jam-packed with news, comment and markets data. There's so much, in fact, that the home page can appear a little overwhelming. It caused a stir when it was the first financial information site to offer live share prices for free, absorbing the charge levied by the Stock Exchange. The site is heavily weighted towards editorial content, in the realization that the majority of UK

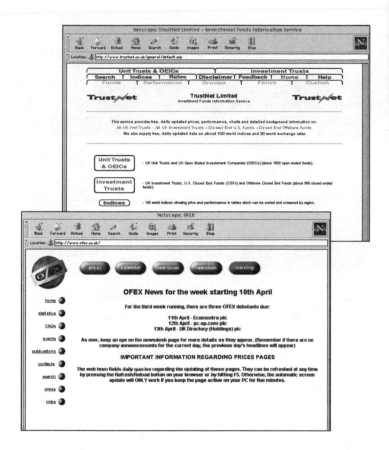

*Two other investment information websites: TrustNet (top)
and Ofex (bottom).*

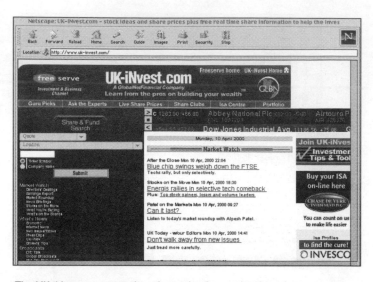

The UK-iNvest.com site is heavily weighted towards editorial content and places emphasis on educating investors.

investors are still pretty new to the whole idea and need a lot of hand-holding along the way. It's in GlobalNet's interests to do this since it is also launching its own internet brokerage soon. It may even be up and running by the time this guide is published. The theory is that the more educated investors are, the more confident they will be and the more frequently they will trade. There are some interesting interactive features on the site, besides the usual news and analysis, such as 'Ask The Experts', where the best questions submitted by users are answered by experts.

UK Online Investing (www.ukonlineinvesting.com)

This a relatively new site dedicated to providing investors with research resources. It provides free annual and company reports from over 1,500 UK listed companies, thanks to its

This relatively new site from UK Online Investing provides reports from more than 1,500 UK listed companies.

link with the **Multex Investor Network** (www.multex investor.com). There's also a useful broker commission comparison tool. It e-mails you all the commission costs charged by each online broker for deals of increasing size, from £1,000 to £100,000.

Yahoo! Finance (http://finance.uk.yahoo.com)

Yahoo, the one-time search engine and now general web portal to the world, is building up an impressive array of business and financial links on this site, making it a powerful resource for UK online investors. It includes news, links to share price providers and online brokers. Yahoo's international perspective means you get a good range of services covering various countries, including Europe and the USA. If you're looking for a global jumping-off point, this is a good site to start from.

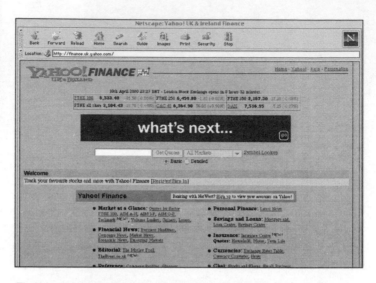

The Yahoo! web portal has an impressive array of business and financial links, making it a good site to start from.

Bring on the brokers!

NOTE ON CHARGES: The online investing market is so dynamic at the moment that tariff structures almost undoubtedly will have changed between the writing and publication of this guide. The competition is becoming intense, and that's good news for investors. So it's just as well that there are excellent commission comparison tools on Interactive Investor, Motley Fool and UK Online Investing. As a website is easier to keep up to date than a book, do try out these sites when working out likely dealing costs for different sizes of deal.

But bear in mind that these calculators don't take any extra fees into account. A broker may offer a really low commission rate but then charge a £50 annual administration fee, effectively wiping out any saving over a broker that charges a higher commission but no annual fee.

Also, some brokers offer lower dealing commissions once you've transacted a minimum number of times per month or quarter. There may also be an annual membership fee in return for lower-than-normal commissions. These brokers certainly don't like to make comparisons that easy. And bear in mind anyway that commission levels shouldn't be the only reason why you choose one broker over another.

The trend is towards a flat fee structure – one fee no matter what the size of the deal. This obviously favours those who tend to deal in large amounts at a time. Traditionally there was always a tiered tariff, ensuring that brokers were paid more for larger deals. But in these days of fully automated dealing, such price differentials are hard to justify. The process is the same whether the deal is for 100 shares or 10,000 shares.

For some reason there seems to be a steep change in charges when the deal size gets beyond £1,500. If you want to invest around that much, it may be worth reducing the number of shares by just a few so that you come within the £1,500 limit. It should save you a few pounds on the total commission. But to be honest, the average investor deals in chunks of around £3,000, and maybe five times a year. On that basis, the difference between the commission levels offered by the brokers is minimal. It's not worth getting that worked up about.

TIPS

Bear in mind that online commission comparison tools don't take extra fees into account. A broker may offer a really low commission rate but then charge a £50 annual administration fee.

One thing investors can't avoid – unless the Government abolishes it – is stamp duty. At the moment every time you buy shares you have to pay 0.5% stamp duty on the value of the deal. There's no duty on sales. Also, for deals of £10,000

Barclays Stockbrokers is the UK's largest retail stockbroker. It is doing a good job of linking its online banking, credit card and stockbroking operations on the web.

or more, there's an extra levy of 25p made by the Panel for Takeovers and Mergers.

Barclays Stockbrokers (www.barclays-stockbrokers.co.uk)

When Barclays Stockbrokers, the UK's largest retail stockbroker, launched its online broking operation in 1999, it did so on the back of an impressive telephone dealing operation. But it surprised the industry by offering certificated dealing only – that is, customers still received paper share certificates and couldn't hold their shares in a nominee account. By the time this guide is published, Barclays – barring any mishaps – should have launched nominee account dealing and online self-select Individual Savings Accounts, and will offer people the chance to invest online in a number of unit trusts offered by leading fund managers. It launched this 'fund supermarket' concept in 1999, but without the online transactional feature. Investors receive discounts on the funds' initial charges if they invest through Barclays.

The broker has heavily promoted its 'Price Improver' feature, whereby it can sometimes achieve a better price for customers on their share deals by dealing with market makers plugged directly into its systems. The service is particularly useful for deals transacted at the beginning and end of the trading day, when the difference between the buying and selling price (the bid-offer spread) can widen dramatically. Where Barclays fell down initially was over the lack of research tools available to customers. It is only just beginning to put this right. Serious investors will have to rely on research from elsewhere. International dealing is also in the pipeline. And for those who like the idea of integration between financial services, Barclays is doing a good job of linking its online banking, credit card and stockbroking operations on the web.

CHARGES

Minimum £11.99

Flat Rate 1%

Maximum £39.99

Maximum deal size £20,000.

CMC – Deal4Free.com (www.deal4free.com)

Deal4free.com, the brainchild of CMC, a well-respected futures, options and currency trader, is aimed at sophisticated investors who understand the stock market and the nature of risk. It offers commission-free dealing with no stamp duty, either. How? It uses financial instruments called 'contracts for difference' (CFDs). You don't actually buy the underlying shares, just the price of them, so there are no dealing charges. You also buy on a 20% margin. This means that if you want to buy £1,000 worth of shares you deposit £200

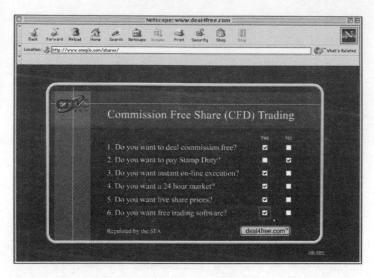

Deal4free.com provides commission-free dealing with no stamp duty by offering 'contracts for difference'.

with CMC. This can magnify your gains, but also your losses, so it's not for the faint-hearted. Profits are transferred to the customer's account within 24 hours. If you keep the CFD shares overnight, you pay financing costs to CMC – as if you'd borrowed the whole amount (not just the margin cost).

You have to have at least £5,000 to open an account and CMC can provide execution-only services only to investors classed as 'non-private'. This means customers have to show CMC's compliance department they have trading experience. Not one for the novices!

Charles Schwab Europe (www.schwab-europe.com)

Charles Schwab Europe is the UK's largest online broker. It offers dealing by computer and telephone (including automated touch-tone trading) and has a well-deserved reputation for being first with innovative services. For

Charles Schwab Europe has a well-deserved reputation for being first with innovative services.

example, it was the first broker to allow investors to manage self-select Individual Savings Accounts online and to trade in options, and among the first to offer trading in US stocks. Most of its news and research data is supplied by Reuters. There are several accounts, the most basic being MarketMaster. Serious investors can join the Frequent Traders Club and enjoy flat-rate trading for an annual fee. If you want to invest in US stocks you have to set up a dollar-nominated account.

As in the USA, Schwab is never the cheapest service around, but at least you know you're dealing with a company experienced in offering electronic trading. Schwab is also spending a good deal of money recruiting call centre support staff, since it realizes that even independent online investors need help sometimes. Schwab's commitment to a multichannel, customer service approach makes it ideal for the novice investor who wants to get serious. At the time of writing it also had a one month free-dealing promotion for new customers.

CHARGES

MarketMaster:

Minimum £15 per deal

0.9% for the first £2,500

0.75% for the next £2,500

0.1% over £5,000

Maximum £75

Quarterly charge of £1 per stock (minimum £5, maximum £30)

Frequent Traders Club:

Flat fee of £19.50 per deal

£60 annual membership fee

Quarterly charge of £1 per stock (minimum £5, maximum £30)

Individual Savings Account:

Minimum £15 per deal

1.35% for the first £2,500

0.75% for the next £2,500

Maximum £50

Quarterly charge based on portfolio value (minimum £5, 0.1875% up to £16,000, maximum £30)

US stocks:

$29.95 for up to 1,000 shares (lower commissions for more than 30 trades)

$0.03 for more than 1,000 shares.

DLJdirect (www.dljdirect.co.uk)

DLJ is another of the US heavyweights providing serious competition to Schwab and the UK incumbents. It brings top-quality backing from its Wall Street investment bank parent Donaldson, Lufkin & Jenrette. You get real-time price quotes, company news, investment guides and all the usual portfolio management facilities. You can also invest in a self-select ISA and buy shares by debit card. DLJ also offers dealing in US stocks plus considerable news and information about the US markets. There's also a free telephone helpline. As with Schwab, DLJ was running a one month free-dealing promotion at the time of writing.

Generally, however, you get the feeling that DLJ is holding back some of its more sophisticated analytical tools – which are available to its US customers – until UK investors catch up and become more educated about the whole subject. Check out the US version of the site (**www.dljdirect.com**) and compare the types of services on offer. You'll see how sophisticated the UK service could become in time.

CHARGES

UK dealing:

Minimum £14.95 per deal

0.75% of the value of each deal

Maximum £37.50

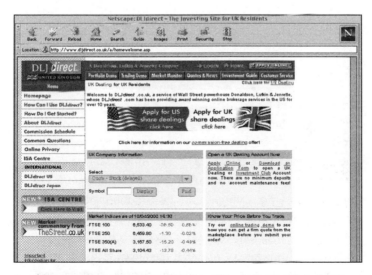

In addition to UK-based services, DLJ also offers dealing in US stocks plus considerable news and information about the US markets.

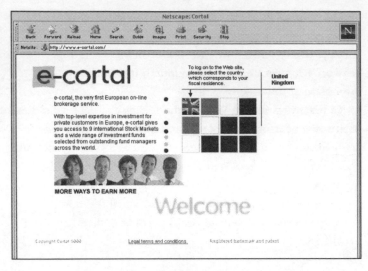

e-Cortal's international dealing service covers nine stock markets around the world.

US stocks:

$20 per trade up to 1,000 shares, plus $0.02 per share thereafter.

e-Cortal (www.e-cortal.com)

e-Cortal, owned by French bank BNP Paribas, is the first of the European brokers to set up a service for UK customers. It offers an impressive international dealing service covering nine stock markets around the world. At this stage, however, the range of stocks you can invest in on each market is not comprehensive. For example, on the London markets you can invest only in FTSE 350 stocks rather than in the whole lot. But this is likely to improve as e-Cortal becomes more established. The range of research resources is also fairly limited, but the service is very cheap given its transnational sophistication. Funds are held in Euros and there's no minimum opening balance required.

CHARGES

15 Euros (under £10) for deals up to 5,000 Euros (around £3,295)

0.3% for orders above 5,000 Euros

6 Euros (under £4) per month subscription charge.

E*Trade UK (www.etrade.co.uk)

E*Trade, another US broker, is aiming to expand its purely electronic service around the world. It doesn't have any shop fronts to pay for, nor does it offer a telephone dealing service requiring expensive, heavily staffed call centres. Given this nimbleness and global ambition it is a little strange that it doesn't yet offer international dealing to UK customers, nor the facility to invest in self-select Individual Savings Accounts. Its research facilities are impressive,

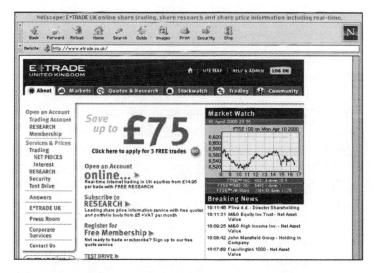

*E*Trade has a thriving investment community and its bulletin boards are always informative and lively.*

however, and guaranteed free for life to customers. You can call up company reports and financial data, draw graphs comparing the share performance of different companies and stock market indices, and get all the latest business and financial news.

E*Trade inherited a thriving investment community when it merged with Electronic Share Information, an online investment information provider. The service's bulletin boards are always informative and lively as investors swap news and views.

CHARGES

Deals £1,500 and below:

Flat rate of £14.95 per deal

Deals above £1,500:

Flat rate of £24.95 for the first ten trades

£19.95 for the next 15 trades

£14.95 after 25 trades

Annual account administration charge of £50.

Halifax (www.sharexpress.co.uk)

It was only a matter of time before Halifax added an online sharedealing service to its existing telephone dealing service. Called ShareXpress, it is very much aimed at the mass market – relatively unsophisticated investors looking for a very simple, accessible dealing service. Research tools are limited to company and markets news, plus the usual share prices. If you're happy to get your in-depth research elsewhere, ShareXpress is a competitively priced service – the minimum commission is one of the lowest and there are no management or administration charges whatsoever. But there's no facility to deal in foreign stocks or within a self-select Individual Savings Accounts. And you can only view your account between 8am and

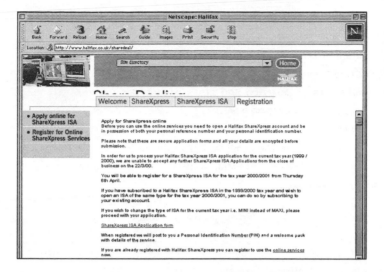

ShareXpress, the online sharedealing service owned by Halifax, is very much aimed at the mass market.

10pm Monday to Sunday, rather than the usual 24 hours a day offered by other brokers.

CHARGES

Minimum £12.50 flat fee for deals up to £2,500

£22.50 for deals worth between £2,501 and £60,000

£50 for deals worth more than £60,000.

InvestIN Securities (www.investin.co.uk)

InvestIN Securities is the UK arm of a small US broker catering mostly for day-traders – professional investors who buy and sell throughout the day in the hope of making a profit by the time the market closes. It offers trading in US stocks to UK investors at competitive rates. There are two versions of its service, one tailored to meet the needs of serious UK day-traders, and one aimed at less gung-ho investors just looking to invest abroad. For the purposes of this guide, we'll just look at the mainstream, far less expensive service. You have to open a dollar-denominated account, but the minimum opening balance is just $1,000. Its flat-rate commission structure is cheap, especially for large-value trades. Research and news is provided via links to external US-based websites.

CHARGES

$19.95 flat fee for up to 1,000 shares.

For deals of over 1,000 shares, there's an additional one cent per share charge.

James Brearley & Sons (www.jbrearley.co.uk)

Even the traditional regional brokers are getting in on the act these days. Brearley's service, called Icon, has some interesting features, including portfolios displayed with real-time prices, rather than the usual delayed prices. But it is fairly basic at the moment, with enhanced services, such as limit orders, promised soon. Its chief claim is on the wealthy investor, since its flat-rate commission is very competitive for large deals.

CHARGES

£20 flat rate no matter what the deal size

£25 annual registration.

Killik & Co (www.killik.co.uk)

Killik & Co is a traditional UK stockbroker that includes the cost of advice in its online dealing commissions. Killik wants to avoid the execution-only route and maintain a personal relationship with each client. Whether this strategy will succeed as more and more cheap execution-only brokers enter the market remains to be seen. The online dealing facility is viewed as an added-value service for customers. Killik specializes in researching smaller companies and less

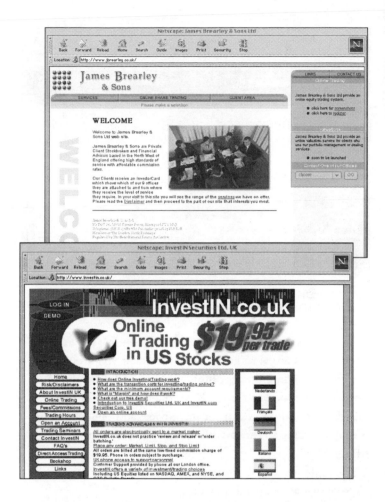

Traditional brokers such as James Brearley (top) are now online and brokers such as InvestIN (bottom) are giving UK investors access to US markets.

If you think you would like advice on building up a portfolio but you still want the option to deal on your own, Killik offers the best of both worlds.

mainstream investment opportunities, and in this regard, its briefing notes are very good. So if you think you would like advice on building up a portfolio but you still want the option to deal on your own, Killik offers the best of both worlds. But you pay extra for the advice, and online dealing is only available to those with at least £10,000 to invest.

CHARGES

1.25% of the deal size, minimum £30

£2.50 compliance charge per deal

£10 annual account management charge.

(Broker-assisted deals cost more.)

myBROKER (www.mybroker.co.uk)

Another impressive new service aimed at the more active investor who is comfortable dealing in shares and other more sophisticated investments, such as futures and options. Share prices are live and free so long as you deal at least once a

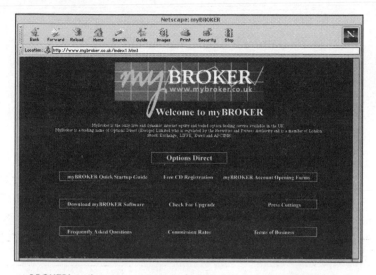

myBROKER's website environment is live, giving you the impression that you are a City dealer.

month. If you don't there's an 'inactivity charge' of £10 per month. The whole environment is live, giving you the impression that you are a City dealer, responding to news as it arrives on your data-packed screen. You can personalize a share price 'ticker' that scrolls across your screen displaying the latest prices for stocks you're interested in. Online dealing in European and US stocks is in the pipeline. You can either download the broker's dealing-screen software while you're online, or apply for a CD-ROM. The minimum opening balance is £2,500.

CHARGES

£25 flat fee per share deal.

Nothing-Ventured (www.nothing-ventured.com)

This is a new service set up by Durlacher, a UK research consultancy and investment company specializing in new media and technology. It's a pretty hip site with content very much focused on the fast-paced world of internet stocks, flotations and technology trends. These guys are experts in this area so the analysis is top rate. Customers also get the chance to apply for shares in initial public offerings of companies that Durlacher is sponsoring. There are a number of excellent interactive features, along with the usual markets and company news, such as 'Smart Agents' that monitor the market for you, warning you when shares in your portfolio move up or down by an amount you specify. You also receive relevant news stories by e-mail. These are early days for Nothing-Ventured – there's no international dealing yet – but the signs are very good. It is showing other brokers how the internet can be used to its full potential. But you do pay for these extra services in higher-than-average dealing commission.

CHARGES

£11.50 fixed charge, plus 0.8% on first £2,500, 0.15% thereafter
Maximum £70
£50 annual membership fee.

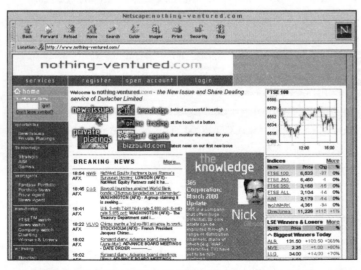

Nothing-Ventured's site is pretty hip, with emphasis on the fast-paced world of internet stocks, flotations and technology trends.

Stocktrade (www.stocktrade.co.uk)

Stocktrade is the internet and telephone dealing division of
Brewin Dolphin Securities, a well-known traditional
stockbroker. Stocktrade was the first company in the UK to
offer real-time dealing online, but it has suffered
a little by not having the vast marketing budgets of its
US rivals. It was slow adding research facilities to its service,
but has since done so, including daily market analysis
from its parent and all the latest company news and
results. There's price and performance data on 2,400 UK
stocks, plus graphing facilities. Stocktrade's 'Knowledge
Centre' is free for new customers for two months. After
that only customers dealing four times in two months get
free access.

Stocktrade's service is impressive for its live share price
environment – most brokers show prices delayed by 15
minutes and charge extra for live prices. When customers

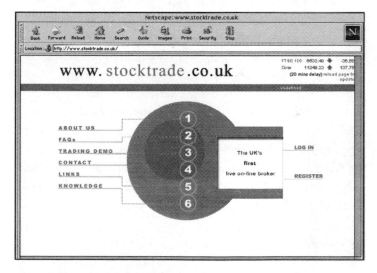

Stocktrade was the first company to offer real-time dealing online. Its site is
impressive for its live share price environment.

want to deal they are offered a live dealing price from the market maker and can decide there and then whether or not to accept the price. Stocktrade customers have to apply for personal membership of Crest, the electronic share settlement system, which means their names stay on the stock register, unlike in a nominee account. Deals are settled the day after each trade (T+1).

CHARGES

Regular trader:

0.4%, minimum £14.50

£10 annual Crest membership fee

Star trader (dealing at least 50 times a year):

0.2% minimum £14.50

£10 annual Crest membership fee

Sharepeople (www.sharepeople.com)

Sharepeople is a stand-alone internet-only broker backed by a consortium including Goldman Sachs and GE Capital. It offers a number of innovative features, such as the facility to deal in UK and US stocks within the same account. You can have dollars, euros and sterling in your trading account. Trading in European stocks listed on Easdaq will be added soon. Bundled in with the sharedealing service is the facility to invest online in a range of unit trusts from six fund management companies, including Perpetual, Newton and Save & Prosper. Investors choosing to invest in these funds via Sharepeople will receive a discount of around 4% on the usual initial charge, mimicking the fund supermarket service launched by Barclays Stockbrokers last year.

CHARGES

UK stocks:

£17.50 flat fee

£25 half-yearly account maintenance charge

US stocks:

$10 in addition to above fee

extra 2 cents per share for New York Stock Exchange stocks.

£21.28 half-yearly account management fee.

TD Waterhouse (www.tdwaterhouse.co.uk)

This is a surprisingly unflashy site from another of the North American heavyweight brokers. It is simple and neat, with some useful features, including an 'alerts' service. You can enter a list of stocks whose prices you want to monitor, and once they reach your pre-set level, you'll be told by e-mail. Like all the other transatlantic brokers it rewards frequent traders with lower commissions, but in any case its tariff represents very good value for the seriously wealthy investor. Other than that, there's nothing much that stands out from this workmanlike site.

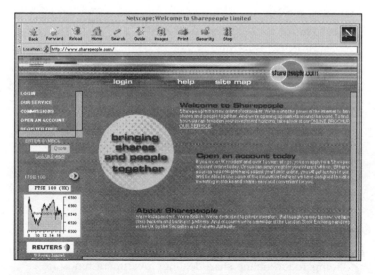

Sharepeople is an internet-only broker that offers the facility to deal in UK and US stocks within the same account.

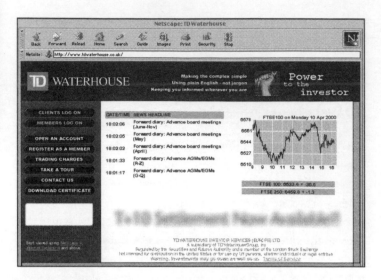

TD Waterhouse's site has an 'alerts' service that monitors the prices of the stocks you specify and alerts you when they reach your pre-set level.

CHARGES

Standard trader:

£12.95 flat fee for deals up to £1,295

1% on deals between £1,295 and £1,999

£19.99 plus 0.2% of the balance thereafter on deals over £1,999

Frequent Traders Club:

£14.95 flat rate for deals up to £100,000

£14.95 plus 0.05% of the full amount for deals over £100,000

Discretionary £65 management fee if fewer than 15 trades in a year.

Investment funds online

Compared to online sharedealing, investment funds are way behind. The unit trust and investment fund industry is still largely paper-based and bureaucratic, so there's not much to report for online investors. Barclays Stockbrokers should have launched an internet version of its fund supermarket by the time this guide hits the shelves. Egg, Prudential's internet bank, launched a similar venture in March 2000. And Chase Manhattan Bank and Investia have announced the launch of FundsHub, a fund supermarket for their customers.

When the Government introduced Individual Savings Accounts in April 1999 there was an important concession that allowed investors to open accounts and make deposits online without the need for a written signature. Fidelity Investments, a leading fund manager, jumped on the chance and led the charge to allow investors access to funds online. You can make a deposit using a debit card. But other fund managers have been lamentably slow following suit. There's only a handful of companies that allow online investment in their funds.

Hopefully this will change with the advent of EMX, a new electronic price and transaction platform for the industry, scheduled for launch in June 2000. Independent financial advisers and other intermediaries will be able to see all the available funds on one screen and place orders on behalf of their clients. Eventually this central trading platform should be made available to private investors. Just don't hold your breath.

Here's a list of fund managers that allow direct investment in their funds from their websites:

Fidelity Investments	**www.fidelity.co.uk**
Fleming Asset Management Luxembourg	**www.flemings.lu/eng**
Johnson Fry	**www.johnsonfry.co.uk**
Legal & General	**www.landg.co.uk**
M&G	**www.mandg.co.uk**
NetISA	**www.netisa.co.uk**
Trackerfunds.com	**www.trackerfunds.com**

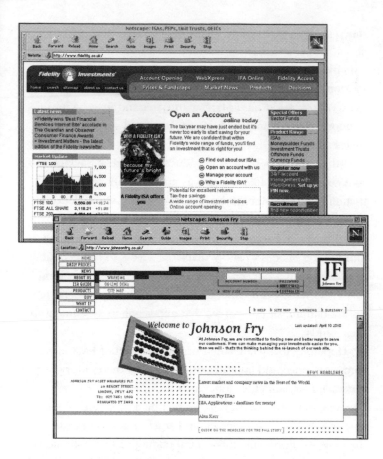

Fund managers Fidelity Investments (top) and Johnson Fry (bottom) both allow direct investment in their funds from their websites.

Pensions online

Pensions have hardly featured online so far because they are generally considered to be too complicated for most people to buy on an 'execution-only' basis. Most people need advice when it comes to retirement planning, so pensions have traditionally been sold by independent financial advisers. But things are changing. The personal pension mis-selling scandal dented confidence in the market to such an extent that the Government has devised a new, simpler, cheaper product, known as the stakeholder pension.

It is due to be launched in April 2001 and is designed largely for average and below-average earners. But many pension providers are already tailoring their products in line with the new guidelines. The idea is that when investors buy a stakeholder pension they'll know exactly what they're getting, with no hidden costs to worry about. For example, the annual management cost is limited to 1%. This simplification will make them easier to sell online.

So far, product providers are only just beginning to introduce online application forms to their websites, with the occasional useful pension calculator to help you work out how much you might retire on.

Interactive Investor (www.iii.co.uk) has a pensions section on its site dedicated to providing information on stakeholder pensions and links to providers. At the time of writing Friends Provident was the only provider that had integrated their online application form with Interactive. But other providers are sure to follow.

When researching pension options online, it's a good idea to find out about your likely level of state pension. The Department of Social Security's site (**www.dss.gov.uk/pen**) can help you – there are plenty of guides, leaflets and links to other government departments on the site.

One company, **Discount Pensions** (www.discount pensions.co.uk) has set itself up as a kind of pensions broker, offering pensions from seven providers so far – AXA Sun Life, CGU Life, Clerical Medical, Norwich Union, Scottish Equitable, Scottish Widows, and Standard Life. It obviously plans to add more providers to its panel before long. The model is much the same as the investment fund supermarkets – lower charges and commissions than you would normally pay if you went through a financial adviser. Discount Pensions offers no advice and commission is 1% with a £25 handling fee on top. Another financial intermediary, Ins-site (**www.ins-site.co.uk**) – soon to be rebranded as Analyse.co.uk has recently launched a similar pensions service.

With the introduction of stakeholder pensions we're likely to see IFAs put under more pressure to reimburse some or all of the commission they receive from pension providers. So be on the look-out for plenty of discount deals on IFA websites over the next couple of years.

Incidentally, if you feel you may have been a victim of the mis-selling scandal, check out the Financial Services Authority's website (**www.fsa.gov.uk**). It tells you how to find out if you have cause for complaint and what to do about it.

Chapter 4

Borrowing: Mortgages

Introduction

B orrowing on the web is only just beginning to take off in the UK, so there's not that much to report as yet. Most mortgage providers are still at the stage of making their websites more interactive by including online application facilities and repayment calculators. Others are going further and giving online 'agreements in principle'. Some more advanced providers will also let you track the progress of your mortgage application online. There are also internet-only mortgages cropping up, whether from mortgage lenders direct, or via intermediaries repackaging existing products for an online audience.

But this is all tinkering around the edges really. The big hold-up is the continuing need for a written signature on all credit agreements under the Consumer Credit Act. The Government's e-commerce bill (*see page 6*) will soon give legal weight to digital signatures, so that applications can be completed and approved online, without the need for paperwork and postage to slow down the process.

But even with digital signatures most lenders are still likely to require proof of identity, such as copies of utility

bills, driving licences and so on. Online credit checking
is possible, but the majority will probably still prefer a
belt-and-braces approach before they agree to lend such
large sums of money.

Another reason why online mortgages have been so slow
to take off is that, for most of us, applying for a mortgage is a
transaction that we make just once every five to seven years.
Once we've done it, there's not much need for the net. The
net is a great way for lenders to market their products and
streamline their processes, but at the moment there aren't
many advantages for consumers – compared with online
sharedealing, say. Consumers will really start to feel the
benefit when lenders feel they can offer better, more flexible
and cheaper products by distributing them online and passing
on the cost savings. There's not much point taking out a
mortgage with an uncompetitive lender just because it offers
an online application form!

Shopping around

Although things may be moving rather slowly on the
transactional side, the net is a fantastic research tool for
mortgage hunters. Lenders seem to take great delight in
making their products as complicated as possible. This is fine
if it means we consumers get more choice, but it's a nuisance
if it makes it impossible to compare products on a like-for-
like basis. There are hundreds of mortgage products out
there, so finding the right one is a daunting task. But this is
where the net comes into its own, because it can unravel
complicated products very easily by sorting masses of data at
the speed of light.

Increasingly, personal finance websites are incorporating
sophisticated mortgage databases in their services, enabling

you to search for specific types of mortgage, from variable to fixed-rate, and to screen out those that don't meet your specific criteria. For example, you may want to exclude mortgages where you have to take the lender's insurance products with the mortgage. Or you may want mortgages that have no early-redemption penalties after the end of the 'special offer' period.

To start off with, here's a selection of the best websites for mortgage seekers. Afterwards we'll have a look at some of the more advanced online mortgage providers.

Moneyextra (www.moneyextra.com)

Moneyextra is the personal finance site of Exchange Holdings, a company that started off providing financial data services to independent financial advisers. Exchange Holdings now runs Moneyworld, another useful personal finance site, and emfinance, an online mortgage intermediary featured below.

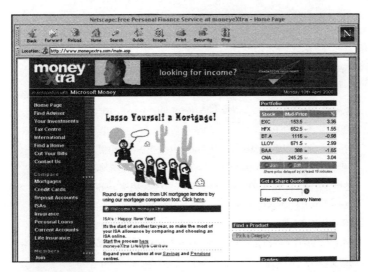

Moneyextra's mortgage comparison service takes you through a list of questions designed to filter out those mortgages that don't fit your criteria.

Moneyextra's mortgage comparison service is impressively comprehensive. It takes you through a list of questions designed to filter out those mortgages that don't fit your criteria. I particularly like the feature that lets you screen out those lenders that impose early-redemption penalties *after* the 'special offer' period has expired. With interest-only mortgages, it can also work out exactly how much your interest repayments would be on the amount borrowed. It's just a shame there's no option to work out the monthly payments on a repayment version of mortgages as well.

You can select the type of mortgage you're interested in, whether capped rate, discount variable or fixed rate. And you can narrow down the field even further, specifying buy-to-let mortgages or mortgages for people with bad credit records. Moneyextra is also developing links with lenders so that you can click on an 'Apply' icon next to the mortgage you're interested in and go through to the lender's site to fill in an online application form.

WARNING

Make sure you read the small print when you click for more details on 'best buys'. Often the headline interest rate doesn't tell the whole story. There may be geographical restrictions, for example, or the advertised interest rate may apply only for the first six months.

Just be careful that you read the small print when you click for more details on one of Moneyextra's 'best buys'. Often the headline interest rate doesn't tell the whole story. There may be geographical restrictions, for example, or the advertised interest rate may apply only for the first six months. At least Moneyextra's database is comprehensive enough to give you all this detail if you bother to read it all.

Also have a look at Moneyextra's sister site, **MoneyWorld** (www.moneyworld.co.uk), for comprehensive mortgage rate information.

Moneynet (www.moneynet.co.uk)

Moneynet is another excellent general personal finance site, and if anything, its mortgage search engine is even more sophisticated than Moneyextra's. For example, you can exclude lenders that impose geographical limitations on their mortgages, or those that only sell their mortgages through brokers. But there doesn't appear to be any way of selecting flexible mortgages – where you're allowed to overpay and underpay without penalty.

Moneynet will also give you the monthly costs for both interest-only and repayment mortgages. When you've entered your criteria Moneynet will also give you a choice over how the results are presented. You can have them ranked by lowest interest rate, highest cashback or by lowest overall cost. This last feature is very clever in that it works out the total interest repayments on the mortgage over the number of years that you choose. The calculations include any mortgage indemnity guarantees, arrangement fees and cashback offered. Moneynet also supplies links through to the lenders involved. **FT Your Money** (www.ftyourmoney.com), another excellent personal finance information site, uses Moneynet in its mortgages section.

E-Loan (http://uk.eloan.com)

E-loan has been very successful in the USA, where it is a major player in the online loans market, offering over 50,000 products from over 70 lenders. Its UK service is a dedicated mortgage site offering loans from 40 lenders. It goes a step further than other information and comparison sites in that it

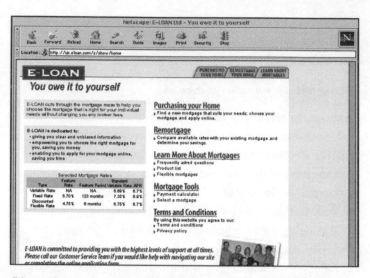

E-loan will recommend the type of loan you should be looking for based on the answers you give in an online questionnaire.

will recommend the type of loan you should be looking for based on the answers you give in an online questionnaire. It then throws up a list of available mortgages and the monthly repayments based on the size of loan you've asked for. At this stage you don't see the names of the lenders. If you find a mortgage you're happy with, you can click on the 'Apply' button and then fill in an online application form. Only then do you find out who the lender is.

E-loan handles the application process and your relationship is very much with them. In fact there's a freephone number to ring if you need help and you want to track the progress of your application. Otherwise you're kept informed by e-mail. E-loan is acting like a broker, but it doesn't charge you commission and doesn't recommend a specific lender, just the type of mortgage you should be looking for. It gets a commission from the lender.

It's a hybrid role that may take a while for UK customers to get to grips with.

There's plenty of guidance and explanation of the different types of mortgage available on the site, but at this early stage you're not being offered absolutely every mortgage currently available on the market. So there is the possibility that a better deal exists with a lender not on E-Loan's panel. But this is one site we are likely to hear a lot more from in the future.

FT Your Money (www.ftyourmoney.com)

As mentioned before (*see page 99*), FT Your Money uses Moneynet to power the mortgage comparison section of its site. But it also offers an exhaustive 'mortgage finder' questionnaire that you can complete and submit to a panel of lenders. They then respond to FT Your Money, letting it know whether they have a mortgage suited to your needs and

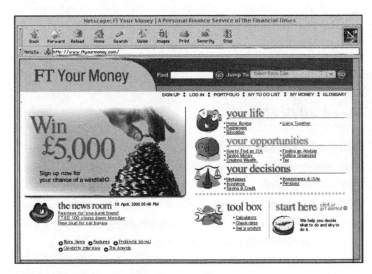

The FT Your Money site offers mortgage-related news, mortgage guides and loan repayment calculators.

whether you're likely to qualify for one, given your financial status and your requirements. Your query is anonymous at this stage. Only when you decide to go ahead are your personal details released to the lender with your approval. The site offers mortgage-related news, mortgage guides and loan repayment calculators. There are also excellent tables giving ratings for lenders and mortgage brokers offering advanced online facilities.

Money Supermarket (www.moneysupermarket.com)

This is an excellent addition to the current crop of general personal finance websites. Its mortgage section carries information on over 4,000 mortgages. And its mortgage search engine uses an exhaustive eight-step process that includes net income entries for self-employed people and calculates total borrowing costs. Money Supermarket also provides onscreen links so that you can go through to the lenders' website and apply directly. The site is planning to add other useful tools, such as new product alerts by e-mail if you want to keep abreast of the market as it develops. This is truly a major force in online personal finance and mortgages.

Need advice?

Mortgage brokers online

The sites reviewed above don't give personalized advice, nor do they necessarily cover the whole mortgage market. A broker can provide a more tailored service, although you will have to pay for such advice somewhere along the line. Some brokers can also bring their influence to bear on lenders in order to secure better deals for their clients and offer products not available elsewhere.

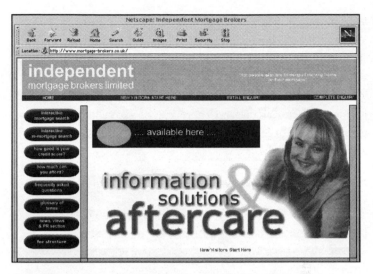

Some brokers, such as Independent Mortgage Brokers, offer online application and mortgage decisions.

There are many mortgage brokers with websites – if you want to see a list of them, log on to **FIND** (**www.find.co.uk**), an excellent financial services directory, and look in the relevant section. But this is a guide about using the web to manage your finances more efficiently, so we're more interested in brokers that can offer advanced online functionality. At present, there aren't that many! Here's a few definitely worth looking at. They all offer online application and mortgage decisions:

Charcoal Online	**www.charcoalonline.co.uk**
Independent Mortgage Brokers	**www.mortgage-brokers.co.uk**
The Loan Hub	**www.theloanhub.co.uk**
Netmortgage	**www.netmortgage.co.uk**
Wilmslow Financial Services	**www.lowcostloans.co.uk**

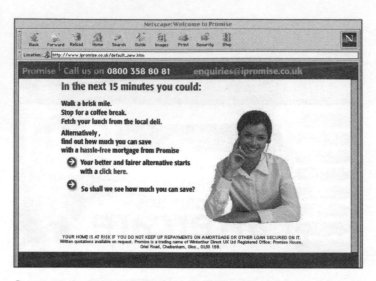

Promise give you a remortgage decision online within 15 minutes. Its simple calculator works out whether you'll save money with any of its products.

Lenders online

As I mentioned in the introduction to this chapter, lenders are gradually adding more interactivity to their websites, incorporating online applications and repayment calculators. But this shouldn't blind you to the fact that if you go direct you're only being offered one company's products. The net can speed things up and help you shop around, but you still need to try several sites to be sure that you are covering the entire market. And the possibility remains that your mortgage broker, who may not even have a website, could get you a better deal than you could get anywhere else, online or offline.

With mortgages, we're not so far down the track that we can see a demonstrable difference between mortgages applied for online and mortgages applied for by traditional methods. At the moment, the main beneficiaries of the net

Market Harborough Building Society sells an internet-only mortgage guaranteed to be one percentage point below its standard variable rate for the whole life of the mortgage.

phenomenon are those remortgaging. It's easier for lenders to make a quick decision with people who have an established repayment track record. For example, **Promise** (**www.ipromise.co.uk**), an excellent service from Winterthur Life, claims it will give you a remortgage decision online within 15 minutes. Its simple calculator works out whether you'll save money with any of its products.

Things are beginning to change, as we've seen with some of the brokers above. They're selling mortgages online that are exclusive to them. The **Market Harborough Building Society** (**www.mhbs.co.uk**) sells an internet-only mortgage guaranteed to be one percentage point below its standard variable rate for the whole life of the mortgage. And intermediaries like **emfinance** (www.emfinance.com) – owned by Exchange Holdings and Charcoal Online (www.charcoalonline.co.uk) – are repackaging mortgages from lenders to make them exclusive to the web.

In the meantime, here's a list of lenders that offer applications and 'agreements in principle' online, plus the facility to track and manage the mortgage:

Egg	**www.egg.com**
Legal & General	**www.landg.com**
Virgin Direct	**www.virgin-direct.co.uk**

Here is a list of lenders offering the first two of the above features:

Alliance & Leicester	**www.alliance-leicester.co.uk**
Bank of Scotland	**www.bankofscotland.co.uk**
Cheltenham & Gloucester	**www.bristol-west.co.uk**
First Active	**www.firstactive.co.uk**
Halifax	**www.halifax.co.uk**
Lambeth Building Society	**www.lambeth.co.uk**
Market Harborough Building Society	**www.mhbs.co.uk**
NatWest	**www.natwest.co.uk**
Nationwide Building Society	**www.nationwide.co.uk**
Paragon	**www.paragon-mortgages.co.uk**
Promise	**www.ipromise.co.uk**

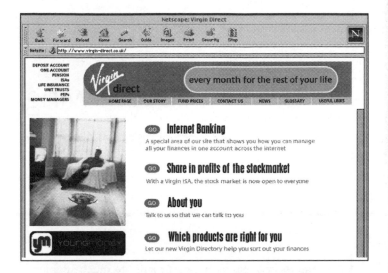

Virgin Direct (above) and Paragon (below) both offer applications and 'agreements in principle' online. Virgin Direct also provides the facility to track and manage the mortgage.

Chapter 5

Borrowing: Personal Loans

The market for online loans is much more dynamic than the one for mortgages because loans are much simpler products. The credit-checking procedure doesn't have to be so rigorous because the amounts loaned are usually not more than £15,000. It's also easy for people to work out monthly payments using online calculators. And as more and more lenders are offering online applications, we're in for a sustained period of intense competition and lower borrowing rates. Of course, this will probably get the Chancellor worried that too much cash is entering the economy, thereby pushing up inflation, and the Bank of England will raise interest rates again. But that's another story.

The web helps lenders market their products more effectively and economically, but it also leaves them more exposed to competition. With the addition of helpful calculators on websites, potential borrowers can spot an uncompetitive rate a mile off these days. This transparency is helping to bring annual percentage rates (APRs) down to below 10% and has provided opportunities for dedicated, nimble loan providers, such as **Easy-Loans** (www.easy-loans.co.uk) to steal customers from under the noses of the big banks.

Dedicated loan providers, such as Easy-Loans, offer online applications and competitive rates.

As most lenders are beginning to offer online application forms for loans, there's no room to list them all. Just look at the personal loans section of **FIND** (**www.find.co.uk**), the online financial services directory. In the meantime, here's a quick step-by-step guide to finding a cheap online loan.

First, compare rates. Try a few of the general personal finance websites (*see next page*) and use their search facilities to find some 'best buys'. These sites also contain useful guide notes and articles pointing out the features to watch out for when taking out a loan. It's important to use several 'infomediary' sites, as some lenders don't supply information

> ### TIP
>
> *To compare online loan rates, try a few general personal finance websites and use their search facilities to find 'best buys'. Don't rely on just one site, as some sites are not so comprehensive or up-to-date as others.*

For a complete list of lenders offering online applications look at the personal loans section of FIND, the online financial services directory.

to particular sites and some sites are not so comprehensive as others or so conscientious about keeping the information up-to-date.

This Is Money	**www.thisismoney.co.uk**
Moneyextra	**www.moneyextra.co.uk** (also powers the MoneyWorld site)
Moneynet	**www.moneynet.co.uk**
FT Your Money	**www.ftyourmoney.com**
Money Supermarket	**www.moneysupermarket.com**

When reviewing the tables make sure you know whether the figures quoted include payment protection insurance or not. If you like what you see, you can just click on the link through to the lender, if such a link has been set up. Otherwise just open a new browser window and go direct to the lender's website. Again, use **FIND** if you don't know the address. It's that simple – which is why the online personal loans sector is going to become one of the most dynamic over the coming months.

When searching for a cheap loan online, try a few of the general personal finance websites, such as Moneynet, and use their search facilities to find some 'best buys'.

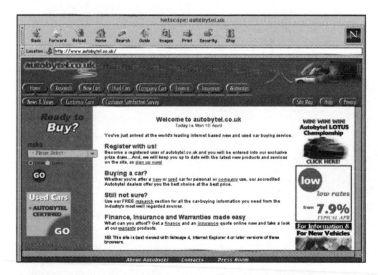

Some car websites, such as Autobytel, are offering competitive rates on car loans.

A few honourable mentions ...

Special plaudits must go to **Royal Bank of Scotland** (www.rbs.co.uk), one of the most innovative of the banks when it comes to online services. It is offering almost instant online 'approval in principle' for its personal loans. Once again it is leading the way for others to follow.

Smile (www.smile.co.uk), the internet bank owned by Co-operative Bank, also offers online approval plus the ability to view your loan and manage your loan repayments from within your online bank account.

There are also competitive rates being offered by car websites, since car finance is the most popular use of the personal loan. For example, **Autobytel** (www.autobytel. co.uk), in conjunction with its loan provider Alliance & Leicester, is offering loans from around 7.9% APR.

Chapter 6

Insurance

Introduction

Insurance companies have been the slowest in the financial services sector to cotton on to the internet revolution – which explains why this is one of the shortest sections in the guide. More recently, the industry has woken up to the net's distribution and marketing potential. As well as existing insurers offering online quotations on all types of insurance, we've seen the rise of stand-alone online insurers such as **Rapidinsure** (**www.rapidinsure.co.uk**), and brokers such as **Screentrade** (**www.screentrade.co.uk**), still pre-eminent in this field.

Perhaps not surprisingly, it's the simpler products that have been most successfully translated to the web. For example, travel insurance is pretty simple to sell, despite the devil being in the policy detail. There are plenty of sites at which you can buy quickly, securely and cheaply online. Car insurance, on the other hand, has been difficult to sell online because of the long-winded application process, usually involving details of previous accidents, no claims discounts and so on. Until now it hasn't been much quicker shopping around for car insurance on the web than on the telephone, despite valiant efforts by **Eagle Star Direct**

113

As well as existing insurers, such as Direct Line (bottom), offering online quotations on all types of insurance, there has also been a rise of stand-alone online insurers such as Rapidinsure (top).

(www.eaglestardirect.co.uk) to kick-start the process by offering a 15% discount to customers applying online.

Two insurers in particular, **Direct Line** (www.directline.com) and **Ironsure** (www.ironsure.co.uk), have led the way in simplifying the whole process and making it possible to insure your car in a matter of minutes. They've done this by being pretty ruthless in whom they exclude, though, as the only way to reduce the time-consuming risk assessment element in the process is to exclude higher risk drivers.

What the web is good for is comparing quotes, although again, you have to be careful that products are being compared on a like-for-like basis. A premium may be the most competitive but only because the level of cover is inferior, or the excess is huge. The web also enables customers to save a quote and return to it later. You can then play around with the variables in a number of 'what if' scenarios to see how different figures would affect the premium.

> ## WARNING
>
> *Be careful that products are being compared on a like-for-like basis. A premium may be the most competitive but only because the level of cover is inferior, or the excess is huge.*

Shopping for insurance online

So when you're looking to renew your insurance, whether it's travel, pet, life, motor, home or health, the following options are open to you online. Firstly, peruse the general personal finance portal websites already reviewed in previous chapters. They contain a wealth of information, from general guides, to 'best buy' tables and links to insurers. Secondly, you can go to an online broker who will help you shop around for the best deal. And thirdly, because you can't assume that the broker will cover the whole market, you should check out a few insurers direct as well.

For each type of insurance, I've selected my favourite websites, chosen mostly for the degree of functionality they offer, particularly the ability to buy online. They won't necessarily offer the cheapest products, however. Some names crop up again and again. That's because there's only a handful of companies really making the most of what the web can offer. This guide is as much about showing what the net can do to make your lives easier, as it is about showing how to find the cheapest products. For a more comprehensive list of insurers online, go to the insurance section of **FIND** (www.find.co.uk).

Life insurance

First Global Insurance Services	www.ins-site.co.uk
Life-Search	www.life-search.co.uk
Lifequote	www.lifequote.co.uk
Life Policies Direct	www.lifepoliciesdirect.co.uk
CGU Direct	www.cgu-direct.co.uk
Moneyextra	www.moneyextra.com/term
Online Life Insurance	www.onlinelifeinsurance.co.uk
Rapidinsure	www.rapidinsure.co.uk

Car insurance

Screentrade	www.screentrade.co.uk
Direct Line	www.direct-line.com
Eagle Star Direct	www.eaglestardirect.co.uk
Norwich Union	www.norwichunion.co.uk
The AA	www.theaa.co.uk
Ironsure	www.ironsure.co.uk
Coversure	www.coversure.co.uk
InsuranceWide	www.insurancewide.com

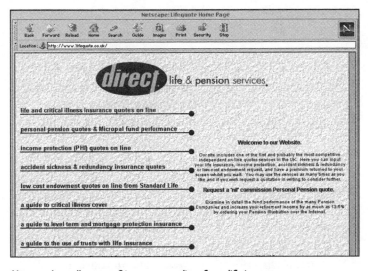

You can buy all types of insurance online, from life insurance...

...to car insurance...

Home insurance

Screentrade	www.screentrade.co.uk
CGU-Direct	www.cgu-direct.co.uk
Direct Line	www.direct-line.com
Eagle Star Direct	www.eaglestardirect.co.uk
Endsleigh	www.endsleigh.co.uk
Norwich Union	www.norwichunion.co.uk
Insure	www.insure.co.uk
InsuranceWide	www.insurancewide.com

Travel Insurance

All the following sites offer the option to buy online.

Barclays Bank	www.barclays.co.uk
CGU Direct	www.cgu-direct.co.uk
Columbus Direct	www.columbusdirect.co.uk
Eagle Star Direct	www.eaglestar.co.uk
Egg	www.egg.com
Endsleigh	www.endsleigh.co.uk
Preferential	www.preferential.co.uk
Screentrade	www.screentrade.co.uk
STA Travel	www.sta-travel.com
The RAC	www.rac.co.uk
Trailfinders	www.trailfinders.co.uk
Travel-Insurance Direct	www.travel-insurance.net

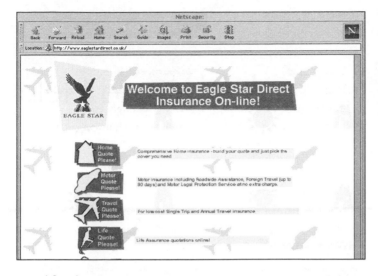

...and from home insurance...

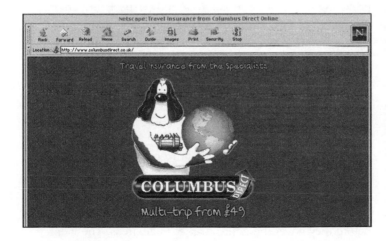

...to travel insurance.

Chapter 7

Advice and Help

Advice online?

We've seen in the previous chapters that there are plenty of general personal finance websites around providing reams of information on most aspects of personal finance, from investment to tax planning. The trend is for these sites to become more transactional and to build up the links to product providers, without necessarily becoming brokers themselves. Personalized advice is probably not on the cards though. The personal finance websites want to become 'one-stop-shop' sites for all our financial needs, acting as a portal to all financial providers. But they generally want to remain independent, if only for regulatory reasons.

Having such comprehensive services certainly simplifies things for net users, but these sites still have some way to go before they cover the entire market in all areas. The ideal situation is for us consumers to be confident that we are searching the whole market in any product category. We want to feel that there's little possibility of a 'best buy' being eclipsed by something better on another site. We also want to feel confident that the information displayed on these sites is

Financial infomediary sites such as This Is Money are excellent places to find general advice on most aspects of personal finance.

bang up-to-date. That takes efficiency on the part of the 'infomediary' and a high degree of co-operation on the part of product providers. Even as they stand now they are a powerful resource for us consumers, putting power in our hands and squeezing better deals out of product providers.

To sum up, the best all-round personal finance websites are:

Interactive Investor	www.iii.co.uk
This Is Money	www.thisismoney.co.uk
FT Your Money	www.ftyourmoney.com
Moneysupermarket	www.moneysupermarket.co.uk
Moneyextra	www.moneyextra.com
MoneyWorld	www.moneyworld.co.uk
Moneynet	www.moneynet.co.uk
WiseMoney	www.wisemoney.com
FIND (directory)	www.find.co.uk

Shopping around is much easier thanks to sites such as WiseMoney.

Individual financial advice?

Independent financial advisers (IFAs) have been in a quandary about the web for some time. At first sight, it seems to be nothing but a major threat to their livelihoods, given the amount and quality of general financial advice there is online. If people educate themselves via such sites, surely IFAs won't be needed to such an extent? It is certainly true that the role that IFAs play and the fees they charge are being subjected to far greater scrutiny these days.

But many people will still need advice, and the web can do a good deal to enhance an IFA's service – give it a far greater reach and help it to offer good-value products. Before the death knell is sounded for IFAs, it's worth considering that they are still extremely important to product providers as a distribution channel. That's not going to change overnight. And those IFAs with the foresight to understand that the environment is changing can embrace the net and offer more

Sort is one of the few companies to offer an online independent financial advice service. More are likely to follow.

sophisticated services to their clients. A few have realized the net's potential for good and bad, and there are some interesting services being developed.

For example, **Sort** (**www.sort.co.uk**) is a new service from an IFA firm that allows customers to fill in an online questionnaire detailing their financial circumstances. They e-mail this off to Sort and receive specific product recommendations in return in the form of reports. The advice goes further than other general infomediary websites because it is individualized. As such, the firm has to be authorized by the Personal Investment Authority (now completely subsumed into the Financial Services Authority). The general 'health check' consultation costs £99, and you can receive advice on pensions, mortgages and investments for £79 a report.

By and large though, individual advice online is in its infancy. As technology improves there is plenty of scope for improvement, though. Once high-speed net access –

sometimes called 'broadband technology' – becomes the norm we'll be able to hold live online video conferences with our IFAs, chat through some product recommendations and then either purchase them ourselves, or let the IFA do it on our behalf. Sometimes they can get better deals for us than we'd get if we went direct to the product provider. The reason for this is that providers often incorporate the cost of paying IFA commission into the cost of the product. So even if you don't go through an IFA you can still end up paying for it one way or another.

But these days plenty of IFAs will reimburse some or all of the commission they receive from product providers if you transact with them online. Some just offer this anyway as a promotional gimmick. Others will only transact on an execution-only basis, just using their influence with product providers to get you a good deal.

So how do I find an IFA?

A t the moment there are no websites that can tell you whether or not specific IFAs are any good, although such a ratings service would be useful. But you can start off by looking at the personal finance websites mentioned above. Most of them have sections about IFAs and guidance on how to find a good one. **FT Your Money** has a typically thorough step-by-step guide through the selection process.
Moneyextra makes great play of its links to IFAs, even including a search engine to help you locate a particular firm, or one that's in your area. It also tells you which IFAs have websites and gives you the facility to include a link to your chosen IFA on the Moneyextra site.

The **Society of Financial Advisers** (www.sofa.co.uk) also has an 'IFA finder' on its website. You can search by

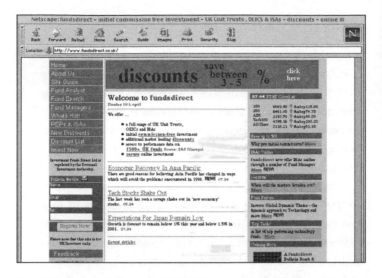

Financial advisers are increasingly offering commission discounts on a whole variety of products largely thanks to the web's low overheads and greater marketing reach.

postcode, town, or by the IFA's surname. You can also look specifically for IFAs that specialize in certain areas of advice, whether tax planning or mortgages. Make sure that the IFA you choose is qualified to advise on the area of finance you're interested in. Alternatively, browse the list of IFA websites on **FIND** (**www.find.co.uk**), the excellent financial services directory. Also look at the section called 'Discount IFAs and brokers'.

A couple of interesting intermediaries worth checking out are **AISA Direct** (**www.aisa.co.uk**) and **Funds Direct** (**www.fundsdirect.co.uk**). Both are offering low- or no-commission transactions on investments, including ISAs, unit trusts and open-ended investment companies. In fact it's on the investment front where most of the discounting and interesting interactive online services are taking place.

Using money management software

If you really want to get to grips with your finances and work out where all that money goes, you could always try money management software. The two leading contenders by a long chalk are **Microsoft Money** (www.microsoft.com/money) and **Quicken** from **Intuit** (www.intuit.co.uk/quicken), both around £30 (upgrades are cheaper).

There's not that much difference between the two and both programs are capable of translating each other's files so that they are compatible. There are different versions of the software depending on what level of functionality you need. And I warn you now, inputting all the necessary income and expenditure details is one of those dull-but-worthy tasks. But with this kind of package, the more you put in, the more you get out.

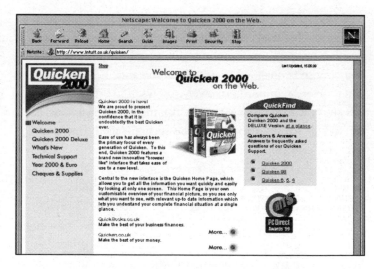

Financial management programs such as Quicken can help you get to grips with all your finance, online and offline.

You can track every aspect of your finances, drawing pie charts and graphs of your expenditure to see what you spend most of your money on. There are financial planners to help you work what products you need to have. You can use the program to organize bill payments and link up with your internet bank, and to manage all your investments in one place. Several online banks allow customers to download statements into these packages, so you can review your spending at your leisure offline, without running up a huge telephone bill.

What these packages are trying to do is interpose themselves between you and the product providers, so that your loyalty is towards them, not the providers. It certainly is useful having all your finances under one roof, as it were. But I wonder whether web-based services are developing so fast these days that software solutions like Money and Quicken may become less relevant. We're moving closer towards a situation in which our internet access will be unmetered in return for a fixed monthly fee to the internet service provider. In this case, the offline advantages of software packages will largely disappear, since we'll be online all the time. We will be in a permanently 'real-time' environment.

We can already manage our portfolios online, so why shouldn't we be able to manage all our other finances online? Banks such as Smile and Woolwich are already offering unified online accounts that bring most banking products together in one place. And personal finance websites such as FT Your Money are already enabling subscribers to store financial applications and answers to questionnaires on its computer servers. Then again, packages such as Money and Quicken have been phenomenally successful, so maybe I'm underplaying their value somewhat.

Tax planning

There's plenty of advice and guidance on tax issues on personal finance websites, with calculators to help you work out capital gains tax or inheritance tax liabilities, for example, plus advice on which investments to take out if you want to avoid paying tax. But if you want to cut out the accountant in your life altogether, you should go for a tax management software program, such as TaxCalc (*Which?* Software, £29.99), or Tax Save (Microsoft, £24.99).

You can do many useful 'what if' scenarios, such as working out the likely tax implications of giving up the company car, or the likely capital gains tax bill if you sold some investments. But the main purpose of these packages is to help you fill in your tax return and save yourself a few hundred pounds in accountancy fees. Both packages are Inland Revenue approved for producing eligible tax returns that you can print off, including any extra pages you may need to submit, and both do the job extremely well.

Chapter 8

Protection

Introduction

In a guide all about money on the net, you may have thought the section on security and protection would be the biggest. We keep hearing that fear over security is one of the main reasons why more people aren't shopping or managing their finances online. The idea of sending confidential data across an open network seems to send some people into a blue funk.

But the truth is that managing your finances is one of the safest things you can do on the net. This is because all your confidential data is scrambled – encrypted – before it crosses the network. What's more, financial services companies generally use the strongest form of encryption currently available – 128-bit. It's virtually impossible for any hacker to intercept your details in transit, crack the code and find them out.

If there's a potential weak point with online security it lies with you, since you're the one that has to keep passwords, user names and personal identification numbers safe from prying eyes. Financial companies know that their credibility is on the line if anyone manages to breach their security defences and hack into confidential data. They will do everything in their power to prevent such damaging publicity.

In short, there's very little to worry about, so stop using security as an excuse and get into money online!

But how does the law protect me online?

When it comes to financial services, we have been protected under the Financial Services Act 1986. But by the time this guide hits the streets, a new Financial Services and Markets Bill will probably have become law, giving complete regulatory power to one regulator called the **Financial Services Authority (FSA)** (www.fsa.gov.uk).

Before, there were several different regulators for different parts of the industry. It was all very confusing.

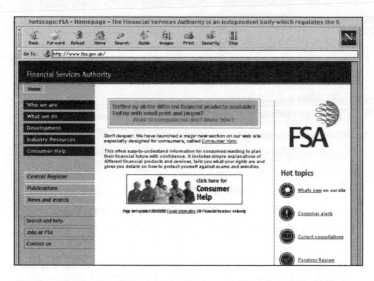

The Financial Services Authority is beginning to take a close interest in all aspects of online finance. Its website is a valuable resource.

Now there is just one regulator and one Financial Services Ombudsman, who will adjudicate in unresolved disputes between customers and product or service providers.

The main point is that, for the most part, the law acknowledges no distinction between media, and the net is considered just another medium, just like a newspaper or television. The transnational capability of the net has thrown up some grey areas that are still being sorted out. One of the main problems is agreeing whose jurisdiction a product provider comes under if it wants to sell its products or services to foreigners. At the moment European Union countries can't agree on a standard and it's all a bit of a mess. But it will be sorted out, that's for sure. The success of e-commerce is too important for all governments to risk confusion and delay.

At the time of writing, the following compensation schemes still applied:

Investors Compensation Scheme
The ICS protects investors in cases of negligence, fraud or theft. It is not there to compensate you should your chosen investments take a nose-dive towards oblivion! It pays out up to 100% of the first £30,000 you've lost, then up to 90% of the next £20,000, making a maximum pay-out of £48,000.

The crucial point is that the ICS only pays out if the firm in default is regulated under UK law. You are not eligible for any compensation if you lose money after dealing with an unauthorized firm. And it's up to you to check this (see **Protecting yourself**, *page 132*).

Deposit Protection Scheme
For cash held on deposit, the Deposit Protection Scheme pays out 90% of the sum lost, up to a maximum of £18,000.

What if I have a complaint?

If you are unhappy with the way you've been treated by a company the normal procedure it to complain to it first to see if things can be sorted out at that level. If that doesn't work and you're still unhappy, you can go to the Financial Services Ombudsman. After that, you can choose to have your case decided by binding arbitrators whose decision is final.

Protecting yourself

When transacting with financial websites, follow these simple rules to protect yourself:

● Stick to well-known, well-regarded websites if possible.

● Ask friends for recommendations.

● If you've never used the site before, check it out thoroughly first. Look for contact address and telephone details on the website. Try them out to check for authenticity. If you have any remaining doubts, don't deal with them.

● Look for sites that have been given a 'kitemark' certificate by an accreditation scheme, such as VeriSign, WebTrader, TRUSTe, trustUK, BBBOnLine, or JIPDEC. These schemes check out websites for authenticity, security and responsibility in the handling of personal data.

● Never give your credit or debit card details over the net except via a secure server. You can tell that the link is secure when you see a closed padlock or unbroken key symbol at the bottom of your browser screen. The web address may also begin with **https://** rather than the usual **http://**.

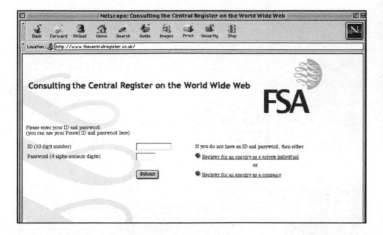

You can check that the company is authorized to carry on the business it is advertising on the Financial Services Authority's central register.

- Never write down or disclose passwords, log-in names or Personal Identification Numbers (PINs).

- Keep copies of e-mails to and from the company and print off copies of any agreements, contracts, application forms or policy documents for safe-keeping.

- Satisfy yourself that the company will keep your confidential data safe from hackers and won't pass it on without your permission.

- Check that the company is properly authorized to carry on the particular business it is advertising on its website. You can check the company against the **Financial Services Authority's central register** (www.thecentralregister.co.uk).

- If a website is offering a financial deal that looks too good to be true, it probably is. Steer clear. For news on the latest net frauds and scams try sites such as **Internet Fraud Watch** (www.fraud.org) and **Internet Scambusters** (www.scambusters.com).

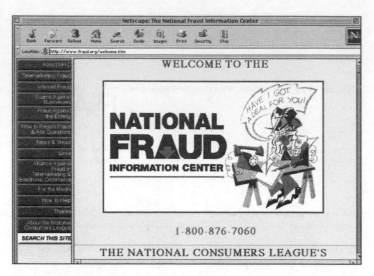

Keep yourself informed about net frauds and scams by using sites such as Internet Fraud Watch.

- Be wary of giving too much credence to views expressed on investment bulletin boards, in discussion groups and in chat rooms. Unscrupulous people may be trying to manipulate markets in their favour. Also, never buy an investment solely on the basis of a tip from someone you don't know.

Index

Acknowledgments

I would like to thank my wife, Wendy, for her patience and encouragement during the writing of this book. She kept the coffee flowing and confiscated my games disks – essential interventions for which I am truly grateful. I would also like to thank Christopher Riches at HarperCollins for his flexible interpretation of the word deadline.

Matthew Wall
May 2000